Henry Ballard

THE STORY OF A COURAGEOUS PIONEER
1832 – 1908

"a time long to be remembered"

EDITING AND COMMENTARY BY

DOUGLAS O. CROOKSTON

This book is dedicated to the
hundreds of descendants of Henry
Ballard and his wives, Margaret and Emily.

CONTENTS

FOREWORD

From the life histories of the founders and early members of the Church, we receive a legacy of faith that all Church members should appreciate and remember. Faith, sacrifice, and service were constantly required and fulfilled in the lives of our pioneer forefathers.

I know of no early pioneer life history that exemplifies any faith, sacrifice, and service greater than the life history of Henry Ballard. Few men gave more for the Church than he did. From his humble birth and challenging early youth in Thatcham, England, Henry learned from loving parents the basic principle of hard work. He was encouraged by his parents to seek an education any way that he could.

With a believing heart, Henry Ballard knew and recognized the truth when the gospel was presented to him. Even with his limited education, he studied and learned the basic teachings of the gospel of Jesus Christ. Blessed with a sensitivity to the promptings of the Spirit, Henry came to know that Joseph Smith was a prophet and that the Book of Mormon was the word of God. Henry's faith in and knowledge of the restoration of the gospel gave him courage to remain true and faithful all the days of his life. Joining the Church at the age of 17, he heroically moved from England to Salt Lake City. This epic event in his life is one that every family member should read, ponder, and appreciate.

This book will help the Ballard family discover the faith and the courage of Henry Ballard, his eternal companions, and faithful children.

Arriving in the Salt Lake Valley with next to nothing, Henry accepted many different assignments and fulfilled them well. He soon was numbered among the very faithful whom the leaders of the Church could trust and rely on.

Speaking for the family, many thanks to Douglas O. and Farris R. Crookston for this fine work. We are grateful that Douglas responded to the promptings of the Spirit to assemble Henry's life history.

May the legacy of Henry's faith, sacrifice, and service be exemplified in our lives today.

M. Russell Ballard

PREFACE

Throughout a good portion of his life, Henry Ballard kept a journal or memoir. His journal is more than a sketch of the life and times of Henry; it is a history of The Church of Jesus Christ of Latter-Day Saints and of Cache Valley, Utah, from his point of view. Henry was not trying to write a history of either—it just worked out that way.

No claim of historical accuracy is made for this book, nor does the author consider it to be a definitive history of Henry Ballard, the Church, or Cache Valley. Everything contained herein is based on Henry's journal, family notes, or the author's observations, with few exceptions, and was written to help keep the legacy of Henry Ballard alive—nothing else was ever intended.

To the casual reader some of the entries may seem irrelevant; however, it is hoped that many of Henry's descendants will find them interesting—hence their inclusion.

Some footnotes are included where there may be other information of interest. Others are noted to clarify terms no longer in general use. Hopefully readers young or old will find them helpful.

To be found within these pages is a saga of how the West was won. In your mind's eye you will see sailing vessels, riverboats, plagues, and pestilence. You will see hand carts and wagon trains in a vast wilderness. Rivers will be forded. Wagons and cattle will drift downstream to be recovered later. You will watch as Indians raid settlers and travelers alike. You will see the effects railroads and telegraph lines had on the pioneers. You will meet settlers in the valleys of the mountains, few in number, living as best they can off the land. You will learn about a people in a struggle to survive against a nation that once tried to exterminate them, and of a people dedicated to their God and the building of temples.

Perhaps most important of all you will watch as their daily lives unfold before your very eyes. Babies are born, crops are harvested, accidents happen, and children die simply because that's the way it was back then.

Hopefully you will have a much greater appreciation for these pioneers, some of which may be your very own ancestors.

This narration is rich with characters of character who came before us—men like Brigham Young, Orrin Porter Rockwell, Peter Maughan, Bishop William Preston, and Ezra T. Benson, to name but a few.

Henry Ballard himself was no less a character than they. All were important in the settling of the West.

His memoir (referred to as a journal from this point on) is rather sketchy in places—consisting of only three entries in the first eleven years. Here and in other places it was necessary to draw heavily on the notes of family members and others to fill in missing gaps. For the most part, however, the story belongs to Henry, and he tells it in his own unique words with his own unique spelling.

ACKNOWLEDGMENTS

I wish to give thanks for the many people who knowingly and unknowingly helped make this book possible. First, I want to thank my Heavenly Father for guiding me to Farris Roundy, my eternal companion and great-granddaughter of Henry Ballard. She offers love, support, editing, suggestions, corrections, and refreshments.

I acknowledge the work of Rebecca Cardon and Myrtle Shurtliff, daughters of Henry Ballard. A granddaughter, Edna Taylor, must also be recognized. Their efforts in compiling and commenting on various aspects of Henry's life offer wonderful, little-known insights.

Lynn Kiel, of Ormond Beach, Florida, transcribed Margaret McNeil Ballard's autobiography into the computer for me. Her work was very helpful.

My gratitude is extended to include Andrea Smith for her suggestions and help with editing.

Without the encouragement and support of my five wonderful children and their families, I might have given up long ago. Their help, advice, and encouragement have been invaluable.

To you unknowns, whoever and wherever you are, your help is much appreciated.

Henry Ballard

THE EARLY YEARS

Chapter One

William Ballard worked hard to scratch out a living in the green, rolling hills of England. It was difficult to do, even for the educated and the wealthy—William was neither. However, William was a youthful, humble, intelligent man who was diligent in his efforts. For these reasons, William was appointed head gardener on the estate where he had found employment. This allowed him to work close to the main buildings. It also gave him the opportunity to mingle with the household staff—Hannah Russell in particular.

William immediately became attracted to Hannah. She worked as a servant and, during some of her off hours, spent time with William. They were drawn together, and remain together to this day.[1] They married in Purley, Berkshire County, England, in 1820.

Life was hard, and poverty became a constant companion. The newlyweds moved to Newberry, England, to see if they could improve their circumstances.

---

[1] After Hannah's death, William grieved for the "Missiz," as he always called her, and was never happy again. Every morning he was disappointed that he was still alive. As he walked out into the sunshine he would say, "Law me, Hannah, another day and I ain't with thee yet."

1

A family followed—three sons: Charles, George, and John. Though these boys brought joy and happiness into the home, poverty continued to plague the Ballards. This prevented even the thought of an additional child. There were six more years of work, struggle, and poverty as they moved to Thatcham in search of a better life. Hannah again found herself with child—a child she was not sure she wanted, a child she felt would be a burden to her.

Thoughts raced across Hannah's mind. There would be one more mouth to feed and one more body to clothe. There was never enough time or money to care for the three sons she had already borne. Hannah tried to solve the problem naturally by lifting too much or straining herself. The problem remained, and in due time she gave birth to another son. They named him Henry Ballard. Later in life Henry remarked:

> The harder she tried to loose me, the harder I clung to life, for I guess it was destined that I should be born.

> They were poor, but honorable people, and many times I feel to thank God that I had good parents to train me in my young days, that I was not dragged down into the sins and vices of the world. I know that many times they have thanked God for their youngest son and were proud of me.

Henry was born on January 27, 1832. Though he may have been unwanted at the time, this was not to be the pattern for life. Henry was more than a favorite son; he was a blessing and a strength to Hannah, and a son she was justifiably proud of.

Honesty, integrity, and righteousness, though great gifts from God, do not always ease the burden of keeping a family fed, clothed, and educated. Schooling was not a priority, especially if a child could help stock the family larder through physical labor. In fact, anything that kept a child from contributing to the family income was viewed as a distraction, and many children were denied formal education. Henry, more fortunate than most, was admitted to the Blue Coat School at the age of nine years. The school was a charity institution specifically set up for those who could not afford to pay. William and Hannah could barely scrape up enough money to secure food for the table, and certainly not enough to pay for Henry's tutelage.

The school itself had little money, but was established to help forty boys become clothed and educated. It was housed in the ruins of a small church in Thatcham. Lady Francis Winchcomb, who founded the school, directed that:

> ...funds should be used to buy bibles, common prayer books and other useful books. The boys were to be taught to read and understand English, to write and keep accounts so as to qualify them for some honest calling.

Henry did well in these subjects. After four years he was considered educated and ended his formal schooling.

Poverty was still a constant companion to his parents. Because of the love he had for them, Henry felt he needed to contribute as much as he could to the family. "Educated" at thirteen, he set out to find employment wherever he could.

Henry found work on a farm as one of several employees of Mr. Northaway. He herded sheep, did field work, or whatever else needed to be done. Henry tells of working with a Mr. Joseph Kimber. The two spent much time together in the fields, and had many long talks with each other. Despite their age difference, Henry and Mr. Kimber became good friends.

Henry had a good background in religion. This is not surprising; he was raised by honorable people who attended church regularly. Also, he had just completed four years training at the Blue Coat School. The emphasis there was on religious study.

Henry's conversations with his friend, Mr. Kimber, eventually turned to religion. Mr. Kimber told of his belief, and his interpretation of the Bible. He was a convert to a new religion, The Church of Jesus Christ of Latter-Day Saints, often referred to as the Mormon Church.

Everything Mr. Kimber told Henry was different from anything he had heard before. Henry was both interested and curious. The new doctrine made so much sense to him that Henry became dissatisfied with his own religion. In time, he was introduced to other elders in his newfound faith, and Henry attended meetings with them.

This relationship could have spanned a long period of time, for Henry's journal is silent from June 24, 1845, until February 1849. The silence is broken with this entry:

I was baptized by Joseph Kimber at my birth place...

Sometime during this period, Henry's heart was touched and his soul satisfied that he had indeed found the true church of God. Henry's simple statement was his announcement of a new life for a new man. He never looked back.

Henry was only seventeen years old at the time he joined the Church. There were numerous adjustments to make, and many were difficult for him. If Henry could have foreseen the hardships he was to endure because of his baptism and commitment to the Church, he may have had second thoughts.

Many people in England embraced Mormonism, but most of those who did not considered it the work of the devil. Priests and ministers of other faiths were quick to condemn it, and condemn anyone foolish enough to accept the doctrines of such a scandalous religion. Henry's brother George was no exception.

Sometime during the winter months of 1849, Henry traveled to London News, a community a few miles north of London, to live with his married brother George. George, along with Charles and John, had established a fairly successful carriage business in the area. They had much to offer Henry—especially material things. George was always kind to Henry, and being eleven years older, felt the need to protect and watch after his welfare. The following incident bears this out.

It was Sunday evening, and Henry had just returned from church. George, curious about Henry's whereabouts, inquired as to where he had been. "To church," Henry replied. George, having already attended church without seeing Henry there asked, "What church?" "The Mormon church," Henry said truthfully. Amazed and astonished, George vocally wondered why, in heaven's name, would he attend the "detestable" Mormon church. "Because I am a member of it," replied Henry. Henry then bore his testimony of the truthfulness of what he believed to be the only true church. George, unconverted, became angry.

George reprimanded Henry severely and told him he had just made the biggest mistake of his life. Henry remained firm, but feared what his older brother might do.

When George could see he was getting nowhere, he enlisted the support of his minister. Three days passed as they tried to persuade Henry to change his mind. First one would pray, then the other, in an effort to save Henry. Henry held steadfastly to his convictions, never wavering nor doubting. The Holy Ghost had told him the Church was true. He dared not deny it. Convinced no argument of reason, no amount of supplication, and no pleading on bent knees would ever change Henry's mind, George took another approach.

As Satan tempted Christ, George tempted Henry—or tried to. He offered to give him the best carriage in all of London. He would give him a coachman to drive him around and cater to all of his whims. Henry would be a gentleman as he presented himself in his fine clothes, kid-skin gloves, and silk hat.

How could Henry refuse the hospitality of George's fine home for as long as he wished? Henry would never have to work, unless it became his desire. A part of the business would be his, and he would never again live in poverty, as his father and mother had all their lives. No religion would be worth losing all this. George only asked for Henry to give up the "foolish notion" of Mormonism.

Like Joseph Smith, Henry kept the faith. His testimony and strength of character prevailed.

George was explosive. He expelled Henry from his home—forever. Henry left, heavy of heart over being such a disappointment to the brother he loved, a brother who had been so kind and giving. Henry was never to set eyes on him again in this life.

Into the stormy night Henry walked, shaking from cold and fear, penniless and hungry. He found refuge in an old barn, and laid a tired, wet and aching body on the hay, hoping for relief, even in fitful sleep. Morning found him still tired and wet. He dragged his weary frame upright and walked on toward his father's humble cottage in Cold Ash, Thatcham.

While he was somewhat welcome at his parents' home, they turned a deaf ear when he talked to them of Mormonism. His baptism was not well received by his family. From time to time his father would listen with some interest, but his minister railed against all Mormons, and against Henry in particular. If Henry was ever to convince his parents of the truth of the Mormon doctrine, he would need a miracle.

England was swept with a sickness known as "The Black Plague of 1849." It left a path of death and destruction in its wake. It struck rich and poor, weak and healthy—and seventeen-year-old Henry.

Although his illness didn't seem like a blessing at the time, it later proved to be the miracle his parents needed.

1849 February about midsummer of that year I was taken very sick with the Typhoid fever when I was brought down very low and many thought I should never recover[.][1] in fact my parents and my three Brothers thought so, but the Elders came[2] one evening and asked me if I had faith in the Ordinances to be healed[.] I told them I had if they would have faith in me although I could not turn in bed without help, it was in an upstair room[.] my father was an eye witness to what was done[.] after the Brethren administrated to me. they staid a Short time talking, and I rested good through the night[.] the next morning I got up and dressed me and went downstairs before my mother knew that I was getting up, She begged me to go back to bed as She thought I had again lost my reason as I had done before dureing my sickness, but I told her I was much better and would Set up awhile which I did for about 6 hours, in a few days I went out of doors and was soon able to go back to my work, but before I went back to work my father went and got baptized, through my previous testimonies to him with regard to the gospel and this powerfull manifestation of the power of God wrought upon my fathers mind so that he could no longer stand outside of the church[.] and he lived to that honest conviction till the day of his death which lasted 37 years, about 3 months after I was healed, my mother went and got Baptized[3] and remained

---

[1] The [ ] have been added, not to correct Henry's punctuation, but for ease of reading. They are used as sparingly as possible.

[2] Henry asked repeatedly for the elders of the Church to be sent for, but no one paid any attention to him. He, however, kept praying that God would send them to him.

[3] When the elders administered to Henry, his mother, Hannah, left the room because "she had no faith in the Mormons." However, she was so anxious to please her beloved son she decided to be baptized.

Hannah worried about it for some time. Finally, she went to her minister, who was of the Church of England, and told him she had decided to be baptized. Knowing Hannah knew little about religion, and especially about the Mormon religion, he suggested he baptize her. She was pleased but said, "Can you baptize me by

faithful to her death which was eight months before my father[.] they both died in my home in Logan at the ripe old age of (my mother) 86 years and my father 96[.][1] they both emigrated a month later than I did[.] they were sent out by the P.E. Fur Company, the first company that was sent out by that company from England,[2]

Henry now looked toward America, and Utah. He set sail on January 10, 1852.

---

immersion?" "Of course," he said. Having great faith in her minister, she consented.

That afternoon he took her to a nearby river and baptized her by immersion; she did not realize she had done wrong. That night she said, "Henry, I was baptized today." Surprised he remarked, "You were baptized! Who baptized you, and where Mother?" "Oh, in the river," she answered. "Who was at the service?" "No one." "Well, then who were the witnesses?" Henry asked. "No one was there except the person who baptized me," she answered. "Mother, who baptized you, tell me honestly." "Well—my minister," she finally confessed. Henry then realized his mother did not understand the gospel, nor did she have a testimony of it. He looked at her with pity, but felt she must be reproved. "Mother, don't you know that you have made a mockery out of a sacred ordinance? Go on your knees, Mother, and ask the Lord to forgive you. Thank the Lord you and the minister both were not drowned for committing such a mockery." Hannah repented and was eventually baptized by the Mormon elders.

[1] The night he died, at the very hour of his death, the grandfather clock in his old home, which had not run for many months, started to chime, as if striking the last taps for Henry's father. It continued to strike until it was stopped.

[2] The journal entry dated February 1849 was not written until many years later. Some of the events he mentions didn't occur for at least 36 years.

LIVERPOOL
TO SALT LAKE

Chapter Two

The Mormon Church leaders, with headquarters in Salt Lake City, were eager to help foreign converts relocate in the Great Basin. They did everything possible to make it easier for them.

People in private enterprise were helping to line up sailing vessels from various ports where "Saints," as they were called, could board ships to America.

Franklin D. Richards was the agent for the sailing vessel *Kennebec*. It had a capacity of 1070 tons and a company of 333 passengers. Captain Smith was at the helm. It sailed from Liverpool on January 10, 1852.

One could be led to believe it was an uneventful voyage, and maybe it was for those days. If we depend solely on Henry's journal account, it must have been.

> 1852   January 10th   I set sail from Liverpool with a large company of Saints[.] 333 on the sailing ship Kennebec bound for New Orleans
>
> March 11   I bound myself out to work for a company [for] two years to pay my passage back to them

9

Mar 14   Arrived at New Orleans after a long and dreary passage of about 10 weeks I Suffered with sea sickness and sore throat for 2 weeks which left me weak

The ship's manifest included, among others, the family of George and Hannah May and their seven children. They were from the area near Thatcham and were converts to the Church. Brother May recalls the 63-day trip from Liverpool to New Orleans.

We set sail on the 10th January 1852 on the sailing vessel Kennebec and were sixty three days crossing the ocean. The Voyage across the Atlantic was a long and rough one. Our food and water supply gave out, excepting the rice and oatmeal which had to be cooked without salt. At the mouth of the Mississippi River the old ship grounded and remained fast in the mud for ten days.

Food was so scarce we nearly starved. Henry Ballard and myself used to go down into the hold of the ship and pick out of the debris, as hunger knew no law. We ate it and asked no questions.

We lived on that three days and then took the oatmeal, cooked [again] without salt in the brackish water of the Great Mississippi.... At the end of ten days and after having three large steam tugs pulling at the ship we were all put on one of them and taken up the river 110 miles to New Orleans, leaving our ten weeks home stuck in the mud at the mouth of the father of water

Henry picks up the story after the 110-mile trip from the stranded *Kennebec* to New Orleans.

...We left the Same day going up the Mississippi River upon an old frail craft of a boat called "The Pride of the West"[.] it might have been entitled to that name in an early day[,] but not then[.] it was chained together to keep it from falling to peices[,] and they kept her near the edge of the river all the way to St Louis where we arrived the last of the month[.] we remained there about two day[s] and our Prest Eli B. Kelsey in conection with David J Ross (both since has apostatized) again chartered another old worn out Steam Boat Saluda to take us up the Missouri River to Council Bluffs

April 1, (1852)   We started with about 75 or 80 Saints on board

10

(Apr.) 4, Sunday we reached Lexington, and the captain and fireman done their best to make head way at this point where it run very swift and after trying Several hours they give it up and crossed on the other Side of the river where there was no houses and tied up the Boat for the night

April 5, The river was floating full of Ice[,] large blocks from two feet thick and two rods long and larger So we could not move any for four days

(Apr.) 8, Thursday morning we crossed back to Lexington the Ice was not floating quite so bad, it broke the paddle wheels some and they repaired them for Starting next day

(Apr.) 9 I was Sleeping by the Side of the Boilers with a young man, James Molton[,] and as I had charge of a famiely by the Name of May[,] whoes father with his oldest Son had left the Boat with E B Kelsey a few days before coming to this place to buy and Drive stock to the Bluffs for our Journey across the plaines[.] finding that they were getting ready to move[,] I got up and went ashore and bought some provisions for the famiely and returned[,] and just set down on some boxes with the famiely and commenced eating breakfast[.] and while I was in the act taking a drink of coffee[1] the Boilers burst blowing away about half the boat taking away the fore part of it[.] killed and wounded about fifty of the Saints[.] the most part died[.] also about twenty five of the others which died. I was blown about two rods and under a bunk with a man with his brains out. I was Stuned and made senseless for about half an hour with a hole cut in my head near the brain[.][2] the sensation which I had while in this position was that I thought I was floating down the river upon broken peices of plank. I finaly saw day light through a door way which proved to be the door by the paddle wheels[.] a man ran past me and I followed him and jumped off on the Side next to the land which did not Sink[,] but I could not stand[.] after getting off I had to lay down upon some boards[,]

---

[1] At this time, drinking a cup of coffee was a frowned on but usually tolerated practice in the Church. The Word of Wisdom was not yet a commandment.

[2] This was a wound that would plague Henry throughout his life. He carried a scar and soft spot, about the size of a dime, with him to the grave.

11

laying there while the blood was streaming down my face from the wound in my head[.] I learned that none of the famiely which I had charge of had been killed[,] but some somewhat wounded which recovered[.] I went back into the boat after I had some what recovered to see if I could find any of my things[,] and I had two sheaperd dogs on board from England but they were blown away[.] I found the bread which I had in my hand[,] also my knife[,] each covered with blood, and the tin cup that I had up to my mouth at the time[,] mashed flat as a dollar[.] the people of the place was very kind to the wounded[.] the fine Steam Boat (Isabel) which was waiting at St Louis for a load left several days after we did, and came up the night before the accident happened, it lay just below us, and they saw the bodies flying in the air and endevoured to resque what they could[,] but very few was saved that was blown in the river[.] many were in their beds asleep at the time[.] it was thought best for all that was able to be moved to take the boat which was there[.] and [they] made the noble offer of taking us free to the Bluffs[.] I lost one box of clothing entirely[,] and one box in the hole of the vessel amidst mud and water[,] which was gotten out after and got a few of the things[,] but mostly Spoiled[.] so I took the Boat again very reluctantly with what I had upon my back and another Shirt and one sock with no hat on my head and no money to buy any thing for my self or the famiely[.] but the Lord raised up kind friends that were strangers to me[,] and give me money to buy provisions for the famiely to last till we got to the Bluffs[,] where we arrived and found kind friends[.] but our troubles was not at an end for a few days after Bro May and his Son with E B Kelsey and others that were with them came home[.] Bro May the father soon took sick with the Cholerhee and Died June 23[.] and his Youngest Daughter also Died on the 27, in the morning with same[.] at the same hour the oldest Daughter Elizabeth took sick and although she was a strong robust young woman just past 20 years[,] yet about sundown she was reduced to a Skeleton and died and we burried her about 10 Oclock that night with very sorrowful feelings. Also took the Same Desease[,] but through the blessings of the Lord it passed off with no very bad effect upon me.

The time of these burials was a difficult time for Henry. He had barely escaped death in an explosion after a long and difficult journey. Many of his newfound friends were killed in the same explosion. His two dogs, precious to him, were destroyed. Almost everything he had ever possessed was gone. There was no money to buy anything and now he was burying friends who were victims of the dreaded cholera disease. In an eleven-day period, George May, his wife, Hannah, and three children were all dead. Henry himself nearly died from the same disease. Of Hannah's death Henry said:

> ...when she was dead it fell my lot to lift her out of the wagon after she was sewed up in a sheet and that was all the preparation we could furnish and buried her[.]...

Henry had grown close to the George May family. He was especially fond of their 20-year-old daughter, Elizabeth. She and Henry planned to marry when they reached the Salt Lake Valley. Imagine, if you can, the thoughts and feelings running through young Henry's mind as he lay his bride-to-be in a makeshift casket and buried her in the cold, hard earth.

His brothers had disowned him, he had no idea where his parents were, and he had contracted his services for the next two years to pay his passage to America. Nineteen-year-old Henry, heartbroken, stood alone. His only comfort was God in heaven and the gospel of Jesus Christ.

In addition, Mormons were not particularly welcome in Missouri, even without a cholera epidemic in their midst. Pressure was so great it became necessary to:

> take our tents and wagons and move off[.]

By July 1, 1852, they had reached the north side of Old Winter Quarters, now Omaha, Nebraska.

Henry was still bound to a company to pay for his passage to America. The company was owned by Lorenzo and Erastus Snow along with Franklin D. Richards and Eli B. Kelsey. Henry, good as his word, drove a herd of sheep across the plains for them, walking all the way, wading all the rivers, and guarding the sheep at night.

Except for one entry, Henry's journal is silent about crossing the plains.

> We met about 400 Soux Indians but they were very peacable[.] after giving them a few things they went there way[.]...

His entrance into the Salt Lake Valley was without fanfare.

> Octr.16 (1852) We arrived in Salt Lake City feeling very thankfull that we had reached our home in Safty[.] my Father and Mother had reached a month[1] before me they having crossed the plains up the South platt river settled in Mill Creek[2]

Later in life Henry recalled his entrance into the Salt Lake Valley this way:

> In October as I drove the sheep down little mountain and through the mouth of Emigration Canyon, I first beheld the Salt Lake Valley. While I rejoiced in viewing the "Promised Land," I lived in fear that some one might see me. I hid

---

[1] Henry's parents left England the month following Henry's departure. They were on a small, engine-powered sailing vessel with only 39 passengers. It sailed much faster than the *Kennebec*. It wasn't stranded on the mud flats of the Mississippi for ten days, and they were free from the other problems Henry encountered. Word apparently reached Henry somewhere along the line, for he appears to have known they were already in Salt Lake City.

[2] Henry's parents packed their few belongings and left the humble cottage they had called home for so many years. They said good-bye to Charles, George and John, their sons. The sons had been unforgiving and unkind to them after they joined the Church. Left behind were five grandchildren as well as William's 89-year-old father. They left behind brothers and sisters and their families, as well as many cousins, all of which abandoned William and Hannah because they joined the Church. Imagine their feelings as they trod up the gangplank of the small sailing vessel, a vessel that would take them to a place of strangers in a land they knew nothing of, while everything they held dear was to remain behind—everything except Henry, a child Hannah, at one time, was not sure she wanted to conceive.

myself behind bushes all day until after dark for the rags I had on did not cover my body and I was ashamed to be thus exposed. After dark I crossed over the field to a house where a light was shining, near the mouth of the canyon, and timidly knocked on the door. Fortunately, a man answered the door and the candle light did not expose me to the view of the other members of his household. I begged for clothes to cover my naked body so that I might continue my journey and locate my parents[1]. I was given some clothing and the next day continued my journey and arrived in Salt Lake City 16th October, 1852, feeling very thankful to God that I had reached my future home in safety. I first went to report to Franklin D. Richards. Brother Richards blessed me and gave me some clothes and a little Money[.]

Henry reached the Salt Lake Valley and the shores of the Great Salt Lake. On two occasions he nearly lost his life, and the journey took more than nine months of "enduring to the end."

But this was not the end—it was just the beginning.

---

[1] After arriving at Council Bluffs, William Ballard, though 57 at the time, (old for his day) shouldered his musket and walked to Utah at the side of the wagon in which Hannah was riding. They arrived in September 1852.

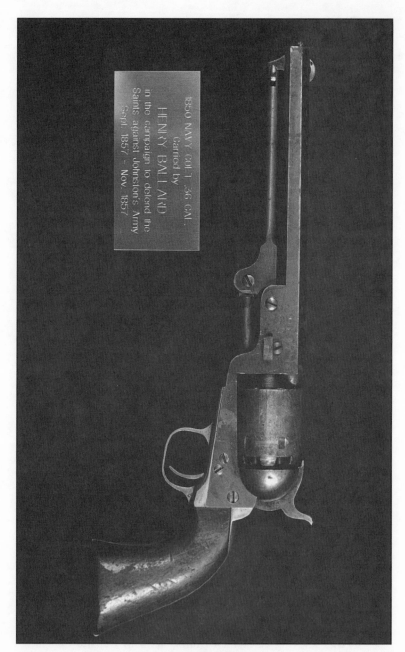

Henry's gun

THE UTAH WAR

Chapter Three

Henry soon found his parents. They were located on a ten-acre plot of ground in what was then called Mill Creek.

The hills north of Salt Lake City were exposed to the sun and offered a little feed for animals. Henry spent the winter there, taking care of the very sheep he had driven across the plains.

> I did not see a soul and I read the entire Bible from cover to cover it was indeed good company for me.

Even though Henry had been baptized, he was baptized again in the Jordan River in January of 1853. To be baptized more than once was a lot more common in the early days of the Church. It was a recommitment of sorts.

He later was ordained a member of the 37th Quorum of Seventies, and in December of 1856 was baptized for the third time. He didn't seem to mind the icy waters.

Henry received his endowments in the Salt Lake City Endowment House in May of 1857. Later the same year he received his patriarchal blessing from John Young, assisted by William Ballard, his father.

17

By the time July fourth rolled around, Henry had become a member of the Utah Militia.[1] It was an organization similar to the Nauvoo Legion, but was not connected to it. As early as 1849 it became apparent some organization to provide for the common defense was needed, and so the miltia was formed. Henry was with the militia that year when they paraded the streets of Salt Lake City in celebration of Independence Day.

On July 24, Henry attended a pioneer day celebration in Cottonwood Canyon.[2] President Brigham Young was in attendance and spoke at the celebration.

> (July) 29 A great light was seen in the Heavens which made it almost like day for a short time[.] Word had come to Prest Young that an army was coming against Utah through lyeing reports sent to Washington by our enemies and the mails for Utah was stoped.

For Henry, this declaration was the beginning of the Utah War.

The Utah War, as it is known in some circles, was a conflict between the United States government and the Mormon Church. It came about for the very reasons Henry stated in his journal. An army had been sent West to "scalp old Brigham."

While it is not our purpose here to recount the Utah War, we should mention the part Henry played in it. He kept his journal faithfully from the last of September until

---

[1] All males in the Salt Lake Valley from age fourteen to seventy-five were expected to serve. Henry was a member for eighteen years, at which time the militia was dissolved.

[2] What a celebration it must have been. It was located on the shores of Silver Lake, at the head of Cottonwood Canyon, at an elevation of 8000 feet. There were 2587 persons with 464 carriages and wagons, 1028 horses and mules, and 322 oxen and cows. Several instrumental bands and many of the Utah Militia men were also present.

December. In these entries he details the events as he saw them. His first entry concerning active duty reads:

> Sept 2, (1857) we were called out to get instructions to be ready to take a campain East to meet the army

By September 28 the militia was five miles up Echo Canyon. Two days later they were in Fort Bridger. They used Fort Bridger for their own convenience, but planned to burn it if necessary.

> Octr 1 (1857) We were Caching up Wagens[1] and Iron and other things preparitory to burning the place when wisdom would dictate...

The next few days were spent in and around Fort Bridger—in sight of the enemy part of the time. Army wagon trains were set afire, cattle were taken, and the dry fields of grass were burned to make it more difficult for the army. The militia men were shot at, they were hungry, they were without shelter, there was sickness among them, and they were cold. Yet Henry never referred to any of these as hardships.

> (Oct.) 2 ...that night Lot Smith passed us on the way down to Green river, which resulted in the burning of a train of Wagons[2]

---

[1] Loading up wagons.

[2] The first U.S. Army wagons were encountered on October 4 and were given the choice of turning back or being destroyed. The army opted to turn back, but as soon as the "Mormon Guerrillas" seemed to be a safe distance away, the U.S. Army returned again. This was more than Lot Smith could abide. In the next few days he, with his troops, burned 74 wagons, destroying the following items: 46 tons of bacon, 1 ton of ham, 84 tons of flour, 9,000 pounds of coffee, 1,400 pounds of sugar, 2,970 gallons of vinegar, 6 tons of soap, 84 gallons of molasses, 4 tons of bread and 1000 pounds of tea. In addition, a thousand head of cattle were driven off. Army Wagon Master Dawson begged, "For God's sake, don't burn the trains." Lot Smith replied, "It is for His sake that I am going to burn them." He then set about his task of doing just that.

(Oct.) 4, We started again for the Soilders camp[,] 40 of us led by Orin Porter Rockwell[.] our plan was to drive off their cattle so as to cripple them in their movements...camped in a large hollow only about one mile from them

(Oct.) 5, We started through the hills to get in above them and passed a picket[1] gaurd and then came over in plain sight of the camp and watered our horses and commenced burning grass only half a mile from their camp...

Oct. 6 ...we commenced our work of fireing till noon when we heard there cannon fireing so we again retreated[.] 9 of us went into the mountains a long way with O.P. Rockwell & Milo Andrews[.]...one of our men (Reubin Miles) had taken sick with the Mountain fever hence we had to move very slow by 2 men going one on each side to hold him upon his horse[.]...could not find our other part of the company and they had all our provisions[.]...had to camp on the bottom without any supper...

Octr.7, (1857) It was snowing hard and the man very sick and nothing in camp to eat[.] I was sent to hunt up the lost camp I went 5 miles up the creek and found them at the end of the fire and 15 other men had come from R. T. Burtons camp on Bear river, we finally all got together again and eat about all there was in camp, that night a deserter from the Soilders camp come into ours, and give us the news of their camp, he felt pleased to find friends—different to what he expected

(Oct.) 9 Bro Sudwicks and myself crossed the river both on one horse[.] it mired down and we had to get off in the mud and Ice and water as best we could[.] we was going to hunt an old camp ground to See if we could find any thing to eat but it was a failure, and I caught a very bad cold[.]...that night the provisions came and we all felt very hungery for we had had nothing for over 2 days[.] ... we then got news of Lot Smith burning the Wagons[,] 52[,] and taking their teams

Octr. 10, We were covered with Snow laying in our slim bed on the ground and I very sick with mountain fever...

---

[1] Picket: A detatchment of one or more soldiers on guard against enemy approach.

(Oct.) 14, I was helping to dig potatoes and burring them for future use,...

(Oct.) 16, We was treading our wheat and cleaning it

(Oct.) 17, It snowed all night

(Oct.) 18, (1857) Still snowing we built us some wickehups[1] for shelter

(Oct.) 24, We were again building Wickehups

(Oct.) 25, ...we soon struck the Muddy [river] and followed down it for some time to find a ford which was very bad[.] we finally tried one place and all crossed safe but one, that had our flour upon his horse[.] and as his horse begun to climb up the opposite bank his horses feet stuck fast in the mud and the horse fell backwards upon his rider and wetting him as well as our flour[.] we could not travel very far because it was freezing so hard and the young mans clothes was freezing upon him so we had to stop and make a fire to dry his cloths.

(Oct.) 26, ...we stoped and got our guns free from our saddles...when some of us got within 150 yards of them[.] they raised and fired upon us[.] I was the third nearest to them[.] we each turned as fast as we could making distance as fast as we could but the bullets flew around us like hail plowing in the dust and cutting off the sage brush[.] but through the blessings of the Lord none of us was hit nor none of our horses nor no sign of any bullet in our clothing[.]...Wm Hill lost his hat

Nov 20 ...News came that the Soilders had ventured to take the ruins of Fort Bridger after besieging it all day and finding no one there[.]...some also went up to Fort Supply and captured that empty place[.] So now they thought they had gained a great victory in having what we was willing for them to have...

(Nov.) 30 News came that our release had come...

Decr 1 (1857) We started home having to foot it which made us very foot sore after being on horse back for the last 10 weeks --

---

[1] Wickiups are crude wood frames covered with brush or other debris.

Henry made it home. By starting as early as 3:00 A.M., they made it in about two days. His stay was short lived, however.

On January 27, 1858, his ward, the Mill Creek Ward, was again called upon to furnish forty-five men and sixty horses or mules to form a new company for Orrin Porter Rockwell—the war was not yet over.

Henry was among those called, and he was mustered back into the militia on February 23.

His experiences were similar to those of the last campaign, only this time he mentioned an encounter with Indians.

> (Apr) 29   The freindly Indian Weber Tom with his squaw came into our camp and staid all night

Henry was relieved of duty, for the second time, on April 30. When he arrived in Salt Lake City, his family, along with many others including Brigham Young, was moving south into Utah County. This move was made as a temporary precaution for their own protection from the army.

By this time his father had already moved five wagon loads and returned for more. Henry, with his parents and their livestock, headed south again. They left the house empty and talked of burning it to the ground, should it become necessary, leaving it as much like a wilderness as they could.

Travel was slow for them, and Henry's battles were far from over. However, the new battles had more to do with pigs and wagons than soldiers.

> May 24,   ... we could not travel very far in a day as we had to drive our pigs which was slow

The Utah War

Slow indeed, for it took them a day to get to Point of the Mountain and another day before they arrived at what is now Pleasant Grove. The next day found them on the Provo Bench where they camped for the night.

(May) 29   Our pigs give out and we only got 2 miles South of Provo City

(May) 30   Bro Bowketts Wagon wheel broke so we had to borrow another one to get to Spring Creek

May 31   We went to Santiquin and got the wheel mended and brought back some lumber we had left there and built us a small shanty

Their move to Utah Valley was now complete. Still, life was anything but routine. Wood was needed for burning, and cedar posts had to be located for fences and buildings. In early June news came saying Indians had killed three men and a woman in Salt Creek, and so the Saints were forced to move closer together for self protection.

Indians were stealing cattle, and they even stole a little girl. Fortunately, the pioneers were able to get her back. However, the threat of Indians made it necessary for the Saints to be with their cattle day and night.

Gradually, threats by both the Indians and the Army subsided somewhat, and on June 12:

President Young and the Brethern met with a peace commision and agreed the army could come peaceaby if they would go to some valley not less than forty miles of Salt Lake City and molest no one[.] they gladly agreed to this...

Then came this important and much awaited announcement:

(July) 1, 1858   Prest Young sent word that all could have the privilage of returning to their homes...

From that same entry comes this happy note:

...I got tired of driving Pigs going South, so I loaded them up
in the Wagon and took them home first[1]...

Henry may have come to terms with the pigs and the
soldiers, but the war with the wagons, if ever won, was won
much later in life. Sometime in the future he could be quoted
as saying:

...I had quite a time with old wagons

Henry's Utah War had ended.

---

[1] Back to Mill Creek.

SALT LAKE
AFTER THE WAR

Chapter Four

Hauling the pigs back to Mill Creek was the beginning of Henry's one-year Salt Lake City sojourn after the war.

> (July) 10 We arrived home safe, and very thankful to again have a house to live in, knowing our troubles had nothing of that pain and anguish that the Saints had had to endure in the past for this was the first time that the Saints had had the privilage of returning to any of their homes[.] the wheat was ready for harvesting[.] we was counciled to hold on to our Breadstuff[.] no Publick meetings was held in any publick parts so as not to create any excitement[.] Prest's Young and Kimball kept themselves in private[.] Cummings our new Govenor seemed to be very friendly to our people

Although army troops departed for California on August 8, the Saints still expected that 2,000 troops would be stationed in the valley. Merchant and government wagon trains were coming in almost daily.

The Utah War had ended, but not the hostilities that so often follow battle. Henry's comment concerning no public meetings, and the Brethren keeping to themselves, implies peace was not fully assured.

> Aug 8 ...the meetings were held in the school house as it was off the main road....

As anticipated, more troops did come, but not 2,000.

1858 Sepr 5 Sunday it was thought wisdom to stop all meetings[.] 13650 more troops came in and camped a little east of the city on their way to camp Floyd[.] the Bretheren would go to their camp and trade with them and work for them,

In the same entry, but on a different vein, he notes:

A very large Commett[1] appeared in the west with a very long tail to it, it revolved around the north pole to the east, got brighter for a while and then got dimmer, it lasted for weeks very plain

It was not until October 6 that another meeting was held, and even then presidents Young and Kimball did not attend. The meeting was not open to the public, but was for leading officers of the church. D. H. Wells, of the Council of the Twelve Apostles, talked on a very familiar subject. He counseled the Saints to have a two-year supply of provisions on hand and:

those that neglected this council that was able to do so would have to pay a high price to buy back what they needed, also that nothing should be said that Brigham or Heber had said thus and so but every one must be responcible for their own saying as well as their own doings

October 31, they were again reminded about the:

saving of Breadstuff.

By December, winter had set in—in earnest.

Dec 1 (1858) A very sever snow storm had prevailed through the night and lasting all day blowing at a fearful rate from the east[.] many cattle where frose[.] and Bro Leaver a tailor from Salt Lake he had come from camp Floyd on the Stage to Cottonwood[.] when he got off to go to the house of Thomas Bullock he fell in a dry ditch filled with snow[.] he was heard by some parties but they thought it was stock and he laid there and froze to death[.] also another man froze to death coming from the West mountain canyon to Wm Hickmans

---

[1] This was not Halley's comet. The Hansen Planetarium in Salt Lake City was unable to name it.

house and several others in different parts, it was said to be the coldest storm in 10 years in Utah

Some progress toward total peace was being made. On December 26, President James Buchanan sent a pardon to all Mormons for "burning their wagons[1] on the plains," and recommended a land office be set up in Salt Lake City. The pardon came from Washington in only 14 days. Not long, considering it took Henry a little over nine months to make the journey from England.

The pardon made the General Authorities feel they could again use the "Tabernacle."[2] It was opened to the public for the first time since the Saints returned from Utah County.

Life was more routine for Henry and the Saints for a while.

1859 Jany 22 I went over to the Bishops house and settled my Tithing, and on my way home my horse which was a young one shyed off the road as I met 2 others comming in an opposite direction, and in doing so run onto the Ice and fell on my leg and split off the ancle bone of my right foot and badly bruised it which layed me up for some time

(Feb.) 13, I went to meeting for the first time since I got hurt[.] Bishop Miller preached to us a good sermon upon the Necesity of keeping on board the ship Zion, for it would bear us through the storm all right[.] I got a letter from my 3 Brothers in England they did not belong to the church and nor no way faverable

Henry must have been disappointed with the news from his brothers—he loved them dearly. He also loved the gospel plan and wanted very much to share it with them.

---

[1] The author assumes the wagons were the soldiers' wagons destroyed by the Utah Militia during the Utah War.

[2] The tabernacle to which Henry refers must not be confused with the present-day Tabernacle built many years later.

It was still touch and go with the troops at Camp Floyd. It takes time for peace, and sometimes it just doesn't come easily. Elections, normally held in March, were changed to November. This was probably done to placate the military, as they were still a problem for the Saints.

...also to withdraw the troops from in around Provo to camp Floyd, as the President stated in his messaage to congress that Col Johnstone should not locate any body of troops near to any thickly settlement in the Teritory of Utah, and to make peace but instead they were trying to do all they could to break the peace and put the Govenor at defiance

Mar 25 Howard Spencer son of Orson was brought home to the City from Rush valley, where he had been badly wounded by a U.S. officer[.] a small body of Soilders was camped in that locality[,] and 16 of them with an Officer Ordered Bro Spencer to take his stock away from the ranch which his Uncles and others had received a grant of the legeslation[.] he refused to comply with their request[.] they marched up in file to where he was feeding his stock some hay[.] the officer, Sargent Pike commanded his men to take him, but before they had time to do so, Pike raised his gun and struck him over the head with the Breach of it[.] Bro Spencer raised his pitchfork which he was feeding his stock with over his head to save the blow and the handle broke in 2 peices[,] one end striking him on the back of his head and braking his skull so it had to be sawed to get it back into its place[.] but it was then thought that he would recover which he did after a good deal of care

And then:

April 3 Sunday Bishop R Miller spoke upon the subject of our enemies coming against us in a national way...[Name in original journal] was cut off for apostacy[.] that the spirit was taking great hold upon the people[.] in the evening we signed a Petition Praying Bishop Brinton of the Cottonwood Ward to have [Name in original journal] stop making Wiskey and selling it, or deal with him accordingly for the salvation of Israel

1859 April 6 The annual conference commenced publicly[.] the first Presidents and several of the Twelve were present[.] H. C. Kimball said that the apostates was more hurtful in our midst than the army,...his urgent call was to save our breadstuff for time of Famine for it would certinly come

(Apr.) 7 John Taylor represented the Authorities of the church and spoke of the union of this people in casting their votes to sustain their leader, defying the world to produce its equal[.] Prest Young spoke of the weakness of mankind, and the exaltation of the Saints to the diferent degrees of Glory

(Apr.) 10 Sunday held a meeting in the new meeting house in the lower part of the Ward for the purpose of Blessing young children and Baptizing those of that age[.] also took action against [Name in original journal] for again making Wiskey after he had promised to stop, but he said that he did not promise that he would not commence again and thus treated the Priesthood with contempt[.] he had been droped by his Quorum in the city, and this day cut off by the Ward for violation of his covenants

(Apr.) 26 A company was called to march to the low mountins to watch[.] the army threatened to come into Salt Lake City and take Prest Young or fight[.] I was called amoung the rest to go to the schoolhouse but the foot men was all released they only needed horse men, so I was releived but could not leave the Ward for a few days to see what may be wanted as I was anticipating going to Cache valley 90 miles North

May 2 (1859) I went and saw John A Smith one of the Bishops councilors and asked him if I could not be released[.] he told me I could go at any time, so I got ready to start next day

This was Henry's final journal entry as a Salt Lake Valley resident, and it marked a new beginning for him—a life in Cache Valley. Cache Valley became his home until the day he died. It was there he became a bishop, and there where he married. There he fathered an Apostle, who in turn became the grandfather of the second Apostle Ballard.

Henry's life in Cache Valley proved to be a blessing to all who lived there.

THE
MOVE TO
CACHE VALLEY
Chapter Five

The move to Cache Valley was a major undertaking in 1859. Towns had been established along the way, but the roads were barely passable. To go around the mountain east of Tremonton added nearly twenty extra miles. With wagons heavily laden and the additional burden of livestock, it could easily entail an extra few days.

(May) 3 I started to Cache Valley Aaron Dewitt going with me[.] it was a new place with the exception of one small settlement in the south end of the valley then known as Maughans Fort, we took 2 yoak of Oxen and some young Stock with plow and tools and seed and Breadstuff nearly all belonging to me, we went 6 miles north of the City and camped near the Brush by the mountains, it was a very cold stormy night and little feed, and the Stock all scattered[.] we hunted for 10 hours on foot for them and still 2 was missing, but we had to move on or we would likly loose them again, so we went on to the north of Centerville

1859 May 5 We took the upper road all the way as the roads was very wet and heavy and feed poor and teams very weak[.] we camped 4 miles South of Weber Bridge

31

(May) 6 We crossed the Weber and Ogden toal bridges, the streams was very high having such heavy snows in the mountains, A very heavy thunder storm overtook us between Ogden City and north Ogden on the Bottoms and we had to camp there

(May) 7 We reached Brighan City Box Elder Co. and staid there for the night

(May) 8 We learned that it was possable to go through Box Elder Canyon so we started that way but ours was the 3rd loaded wagon going up that Spring, the roads was very bad[.] we often got Stalled, we mired in Box Elder valley and broke our Wagon tounge and then [had] to unload some of our load[.] we then got out and took part of our load to the top of the hill and then took the fore part of the Wagon and brought up the other part of our load and camped on the top of the hill north of the little valley[1]

(May) 9 We reached the South end of the valley 3 miles south of Maughans Fort and Camped.

Henry and Aaron took seven days going from Salt Lake City to within three miles of Maughans Fort[2] where they met and talked with Bishop Peter Maughan.

Bishop Maughan had been directing the new settlers in the valley. He advised Henry and Aaron to go on to Spring Creek[3] and locate there. At Blacksmiths Fork River they camped for the night. A church farm was located there, and had been enclosed for protection from the Indians. Indians were plentiful in Cache Valley.

Arriving at Spring Creek on May 11, Henry and Aaron were happy for a little rest—and little it was. That same day they planted what seed they had because it was getting late in the season. No mention is made of where they planted. The next day they began searching for land to claim as their own.

---

[1] Mantua is now located in the little valley he refers to. The 'top of the hill' Henry mentions is probably near Dry Lake, at the head of Wellsville and Sardine canyons.

[2] Maughans Fort has since been renamed Wellsville.

[3] Now known as Providence.

They were told it had all been claimed by the few people already settled there.

The following morning it was so windy it was difficult to keep the cover on the wagon. In spite of the wind, Henry continued to look for ground. He located a piece that looked easy to fence and was located between two branches of a spring. It was not rich ground, but would be easy to break and irrigate if water was routed down an old stream bed from Spring Creek. However:

> Some laughed at me for taking it that way but I succeed alright.
>
> (May) 14 We commenced plowing
>
> (May) 18 Heard that the big wind had blew down the court house in Brigham City

The balance of May was spent sowing grain and planting garden seed. They were anxious, for the ground was getting quite dry. Luckily, it did rain toward the end of the month.

The Mormons were still not free from the influence of the federal troops.

> (May) 27 Bishop P Maughan came over and held a meeting laying before us our conditions, as the Soilders had been killing some Indians near Fort Bridger east[.] also a report that there was a camp of Soilders on the North of the valley and the Indians was mad with all the whites[.] he thought we had better move our camp over to the church farm where we would be away from the willows[1] so they could not ambush us

Since the settlers could not farm during this time, they spent the next couple of days getting timbers to make a bridge over Blacksmith Fork River.

Indians were still a concern.

> (May) 30 We all moved over to the church farm, the settlers north of us at Summit Creek[2] 10 miles north, they all moved to Maughans Fort

---

[1] In the 1800s, Cache Valley was called Willow Valley.

[2] Summit Creek is now called Smithfield.

Henry had not yet located a parcel of ground completely to his liking, and the next few days were spent looking for better land.

> June 2 I went to Logan with some other Bretheren to look at the county[.] we found some good land there[.] I expected to go some where before locating permanently but I thought it was the best I could do to hurry and get my seed into the ground some where so I could get seed for another year with out having to haul it so far

On June 7, he traveled to Shumway[1] to look at more land. It was good land, but there wasn't much water for it.

Looking was a time-consuming job, and it kept Henry from planting other land. This must have worried him some, as it was already late in the season. A crop was not only desirable, it was necessary for survival.

The balance of June he spent working on canyon roads, logging, and searching for land.

> (June) 20 John H. Clark and myself went over Logan river to look again for some land, we had quite a time getting over the river, we staid all night

> (June) 21 We took a claim of 20 acres each, all that was allowed

> (June) 25 I went up the Canyon with Brother Lane where we had made the road into, but every body was afraid to go into it[.] after it was made we got a good load of house logs each, the first that had been taken out, it was very rough and rockey[.] next day the place was crowded and continued so for many days

He spent much of July searching for better land, surveying what he had, and moving logs to where he thought he might build a house.

During this time he received a letter from his parents— his first since coming to Cache Valley.

> (July) 11 I went over to Maughans fort and answered my letter.

---

[1] Mendon.

Henry did take a little time for recreation.

(July) 23 Aaron Dewitt and myself went to the mountains on a Pick nick Servise berring[1] and on the road home we where overtaken by a thunder storm which made us wet through and every thing we had in the Wagon at home was wet

The next day Henry went to Summit Creek in search of some good hay, and from there he traveled to what is now Richmond—still searching. He was invited to settle there permanently, but declined. Instead, he continued to explore the county. He returned to Logan on July 26, and found:

...Servayers laying out the fort in a different shape so we had to move our logs again onto our new lots

By now, Henry was beginning to feel like Logan would be his new home.

(July) 27 We drew our lots[.] I now concluded to stop in Logan for the present at least, not finding a better place where there was any settlers so I got my logs and commenced to build my house

In July of 1859, Henry officially settled in Cache Valley.

---

[1] By "Servise berring" Henry refers to the process of picking Service Berries.

INDIANS!
WAGONS!
WEATHER!

Chapter Six

Indians: Henry's first two years in the valley were challenging. Indians were a problem from the start and continued to bring trouble from time to time.

Wagons: At the most inconvenient times and places they broke down, and they always seemed to be a problem. Generally this caused some personal hardship for Henry.

Weather: This stuff is always more noticeable when you are out in it. Henry spent most of his life outside, and he had a lot of experience with bad weather.

Never complaining, he merely notes the events.

(Aug.) 4   A large number of Indians came and camped at Blacksmiths fork, they brought with them several head of mules and American horses and cattle and Jewelery and money supposed to be taken from a Calafornia emigrant train which they had murdered in revenge for their number which the Soilders had killed of their men

(Aug.) 13   The Indians had a fight with U.S. troops in Box Elder Canyon[.] there was but little done with the exception of the Troops killing a freindly boy Indian belonging to Bro Hunsuker in Box Elder valley the Indians also took about $1000 worth of property belonging to Bro Hunsuker

(Aug.) 14 The Indians all left our Settlements and went into the mountains[.] we commenced to guard our stock nights but the Indians stole some 15 head of horses from Maughans fort and the church farm and shot 2 or 3 more

(Aug.) 31 (1859) We received a letter from Prest Young requesting us to keep a vigilent guard over our famielies and stock & hay & grain and to go to the Canyons in numbers sufficent for protection and hoped the past would be sufficent to learn us to be vigilent[.] glad to know that it had been no worse and no lives lost, a meeting was held in the evening and agreed to carry out the instructions, and to hunt up next day every animal around Logan

(Sept.) 1 We hunted up all our stock and herded them days and guarding them nights

The night and day vigil, made necessary by the Indians, caused enough trouble; the wagons added even more.

(Aug.) 8 I got Stalled with about 20 green poles on the Wagon, and broke the Ox yoake all to peices

(Sept.) 8 Broke my wagon Wheel all to peices[.] the tire run of[f]

(Sept.) 9 Borrowed a Wagon to get my load of Wheat home, and broke one Wheel of[f] that[.] I had quite a time with old wagons

(Sept.) 11 I borrowed a big wagon of the Garr boys and as soon as we had got our load on, it commenced raining and the stock was continually getting into our grain so we had to herd it day and night till we got it hauled[,] and we was out of flour and the most of camp we lived upon green corn and Potatoes and turnips for days together, and was glad to get plenty of them[.] it rained every day till 25th which brought quite a frost, but we had to keep hauling our corn

Henry did have "quite a time with old wagons" and he had quite a time with weather as well.

(Sept.) 25 I examined my oat stack and found it wet nearly all the way through[.] I then took it to peices and set it out to dry

(Sept.) 27 It rained again through the night and snowed in the mountains

(Sept.) 28 Still Stormy and cold the snow reaching to the foot of the mountains

Henry left for Salt Lake City on October 2 to get wagon parts. The trip was timed to coincide with the 1859 October general conference.

(Oct.) 2 I hitched on 2 yoak of Oxen onto Bro Dilley's wagon and team to go to Salt Lake to my Fathers to get another wagon and stuff to mend the old one...

1859 Octr 3 Aaron Dewitt and myself got tired traveling with Bro Dilley[.] we packed our Blankets on our Oxen and took it on foot, riding them over the Streams[.] we took the lower road and camped on the Weber at a Brothers house[.] he was very kind to us, and let us put our Oxen into his feild

Traveling this way, they reached Kays Creek[1] the night of October 4. They arrived at his parents' home in Mill Creek the next day. The distance from Logan to Salt Lake City was covered in just three days.

October conference began on the sixth, but Henry was too exhausted to attend the first session. However:

(Oct.) 7 I attended conference had a good time[.] Prest Young spoke upon the unity of the faith and to be Obedient to the word of the Lord, he felt well and calm[.] H. C. Kimball spoke upon his old text upon being united to the truth[.] D. H. Wells spoke upon home manufacture while goods were plenty and make and sell them a little cheaper than the imported. John Taylor spoke at length upon the rotten systems of men, showing how they had broken the laws of God and Changed his ordinances

(Oct.) 8 Prest Young spoke upon the folly of some Bretheren running to their Bishops to ask every little thing of small moment...

---

[1] Kays Creek is located in the Kaysville-Layton area.

39

The next few days in Salt Lake City he spent trying to do a little trading, but merchants hesitated to take produce. They preferred cash—Henry had none.

Henry and Aaron started back to Logan on October 17; five days later they were home.

The return trip prompted Henry to make the following entry. It later proved to be quite significant.

> (Oct.) 20 Started a little after sunrise, and as we come to the hub of the road, one coming from north Ogden and the other across the bottoms, we met Bro Thomas McNeil and famiely who had just come across the plains and was going to Cache to hunt him a home[.] he was pleased to learn we were going to that place, and we was equaly pleased of the company,...

Henry and James Denning went to Brigham City to have a grist[1] of grain ground. It was a cold October 26, with the wind blowing near hurricane force, and:

> we were forced to spend the night in the mill

It took them from daylight until after dark to return to Logan the following day.

Henry continues:

> (Nov.) 6 Sunday, the Seventies held a meeting in the morning[.] Israel J Clark was appointed to preside over the Scatering Quorums on the east side of the valley[,] and in the evening the Sacrament was administered for the first time in this settlement and we agreed to turn out the following week and get Logs to build a Schoolhouse

The Church had existed in Logan for some time, and now the first blessing of the sacrament had taken place. Wards were not yet formed, but they were soon to come.

---

[1] Grist is an old English word meaning ground grain or grain to be ground.

Ezra T. Benson,[1] one of the Twelve Apostles, moved to Cache Valley to oversee Church affairs there.

(Nov.) 10 (1859)   very stormy so we could not get to the Canyon[.] Orson Hyde, Ezra T. Benson[,] Lorenzo Snow, Bishop P Maughan came to our settlement and Organized it, giving us Wm B Preston to be our Bishop, and called four from here towards forming a high council which they organized in Cache valley[,] and Bishop P Maughan was sustained as President of the whole valley[.] six settlements were now organized[.] Lorenzo Snow staid and preached us in the evening upon the duties of the Saints and their privilages [;] that we came upon this earth to be saviours of men, and exhorted us to be faithful[.] General West from Ogden and others came the same day and organized the Malitia

Jany 8 (1860)   Sunday we held a testimony metting[,] 2 or 3 ariseing to their feet at a time, all feeling desious of bearing testimony

(Jan.) 12   At our Thursday night meeeting the Devil tryed to brake up our meeting by opperateing through Bro...[Name in original journal] who had been deranged in his mind for some months

(Jan.) 19   He tried again at our next week night meeting

(Jan.) 22   Bishop Preston reproved the people for their negligence in sending their children to school now we had a house to send them to, and the trustees had been laboring all week to get a school started with very little success

Bishop Preston would not be denied.

(Jan.) 23   A school was started and the most of the children was in attendance

The missionary system was in place, as were the fast offering and welfare systems.

(Feb) 2   The missionaries went on to the 2 settlements north namely, Smithfield & Richmond[.] we held our fast meeting and brought in our fast donations, also some provisions for Bro Haywood

---

[1] The great-grandfather of Church President Ezra Taft Benson.

(Feb.) 3   We met at the bishops house and took into concideration the case of Bro Wilks which was destitute of Provisions[.] we took up a donation for him which was very liberal under our circumstances

Henry chose to go to Salt Lake City to bring his parents to Cache Valley in mid-February—usually the coldest time of year in northern Utah.

1860 Feby 9 I started down to Mill Creek intending to bring my Father and Mother up with me[.] the snow was 16 inches deep where I had to go over the Devide on the West going to Box Elder Co. I had 3 Yoak of oxen and a load of hay to feed with going down and some to leave on the road to feed with coming back[.] the wind kept blowing hard filling up the tracts[.] I had to camp in the Mountains all alone as I could not see my way to go any farther for the snow blowing so bad

(Feb.) 10 I got to Calls fort which was empty and very lonely yet I was very pleased to find a place of shelter

(Feb.) 11 I reached the Ogden bottoms and stoped for a short time at P.G. Taylors but his stock broke out, and I could not keep them away from my hay so I had to hitch up and drive on farther until I got away from his stock

(Feb.) 13 Reached home[1] found them both well, myself and team very tired traveling 100 miles in the dead of Winter through so much snow

Henry spent the next few days running errands for himself and attending church meetings. His father's well needed some attention; he took care of that also.

On February 22, Henry, his father, Aaron Dewitt, and a young lady named Sarah Hardiman started back to Cache Valley. His mother remained in Salt Lake City until spring.

Returning by the same route, they camped at Hot Springs, south of Willard. The following night they stayed at Crystal Springs, near present-day Honeyville.

[1] The home of his parents in Mill Creek.

At Brigham City they learned the snow over the hill was very deep—so deep that part of their belongings would have to be left at Brother Gilbert's.

On March 5, Henry started back to Brigham City to get what they had left behind, but the snow was so bad he could only get as far as Mendon.

Pushing on to Brigham City the next day, he picked up the things they had left at Brother Gilbert's and started back. The return trip was a trying one.

(Mar.) 8 I started and went 2 miles and broke my sledge [sleigh][.] I went to a house and borrowed some tools and fixed it up again and when I got to the warm springs I got stalled on the dry ground so I had to unload part of it to get over[.] I then went on to the springs and Watered and then started over the mountain but soon found a man with his family stalled with his team[.] I helped him out and got him over to the cottonwood hollow[1] out of danger and left him, I then went on to Mendon to get feed for my team and reached there at 11 P.M. nearly frozen

In spite of his late night arrival and being "nearly frozen," Sunday morning Henry was in church. The instructions they received that day leave little doubt as to the influence the Church exercised over the temporal affairs of the Saints.

(Mar.) 9 Sunday, President Maughan and Jesse Fox and Several other Bretheren came an layed before us the necesity of having A City plot laid off and Jesse W Fox had been instructed by Prest Young to come up and lay of[f] Cities[.] Settlers were coming every day going to differant Settlements...

(Mar.) 13 The Servayors commenced to lay off the City plot[.] the most of the houses and yards had to be moved

(Mar.) 25 Sunday, Bro E.T. Benson and Prest Maughan came and held meeting[.] Bro Benson spoke very Incourageing upon

---

[1] There is a hollow filled with cottonwood and willow trees just before the road crosses the divide into Cache Valley. The little town of Beaver Dam is now located there.

the Parable of the ten virgins[.] Said the wise had done works of reighteousness worth recording but the foolish ones done nothing very good to record nor nothing very bad[.] He had come up to Settle amongst us[.] he brought up a number of fruit trees to plant out

Mar 26 He looked him out some City lots and we all turned out in mass, and fenced it in with a willow fence in readiness to plant out the trees as soon as the ground was dry enough...

Sunday mornings were always of interest to Henry.

(Apr.) 15 Sunday Prest Maughan stated that Prest Young had said dureing the conference that the church was of the same age as Jesus Christ was when he commenced his ministery in the flesh[.] and the Jews was forty years traveling in the Wilderness, often crossing their tracks before they reached the promised land, and this church had been traveling 30 years often crossing their tracks, and in less than forty they would cross the river Jordan to the promised land[.] also said that Prest Young stated that Cache valley was able to Sustain 200,000 people

The problem of Indian raids continued. Henry states:

(Apr.) 29 E.T. Benson brought a part of his famiely[.] he toel us that the Indians had stolen horses on the other side of the valley and they were somewhat hostile in their feelings[.] we Organized a company of minute men to be ready to go to any point when needed

Henry, as would be expected, was a member of that militia.

By now Logan City was surveyed and most of the houses moved. Now the settlers attended to the problem of city water and irrigation water.

(Mar.) 27 We commenced grading down the side hill and digging a water ditch, to supply the city and water our land

(May) 16 Working again on our big ditch to water our farms

(May) 17 We got water into the ditch

(May) 18 The water got half way through the city when the ditch broke washing a big hole in the ditch[.] we got it fixed up and again turned the water in[1]

(May) 22 working again at the ditch[.] the weather was very dry

With the water situation well in hand, Henry turned his talents to other things, such as working on a bower for a place to hold meetings.

Presidents Young, Kimball, Wells, and some of the Twelve paid a visit to Logan. They also traveled north to the other settlements for a few days, then returned to Logan. President Young encouraged the Saints about their duties in their new country.

Perhaps Logan was feeling somewhat tamed by this time, but the settlers were soon reminded it was still a frontier.

(June) 12 An express came from Wellsville from Prest Maughan that all the Indians had been ordered to come into this valley by the Indian agent Dr. Forney to make a treaty with them, and none of us was to go into the canyons till they had settled the treaty[.] the Bretheren drove a Black Bear into the City and killed it

(June) 29 I was guarding a prisoner with others, in the schoolhouse[,] by the name of David Skens a horse theif

By July 22, E. T. Benson had been elected colonel of the militia. Henry's mother had moved from Salt Lake City

---

[1] Years later Lyman Martineau said this about it. "We got the water into our ditch and when it got nearly through the town, it broke and all citizens turned out to help fix it.

"We tried every way possible to repair it, without turning out the water. But just as fast as we put brush and dirt into the break it would be washed out.

"Finally Bishop Ballard jumped into the breach and commanded us to fill in brush and dirt above him, which we did and it was only through Bishop Ballard's presence of mind that the break was repaired without turning off the water."

to Logan with Henry's help. He sat up all night with his sick friend George Watson. He guarded the city at night, and in his spare time he managed to squeeze in a trip to Brigham City to get another grist of grain ground.

By July 23 the Indians were causing problems again.

(July) 23 News came from Smithfield now the next settlement north, that the Indians had killed 2 of our Bretheren at that place, and wounded 3 others, a guard was hastily sent out to guard our young stock on Bear river, also the City guard increased

The Saints believed in a lively Pioneer Day celebration. July 24, 1860, may have been Logan's liveliest yet.

(July) 24 The Horse company of minute men started to Smithfield and came back in the evening with an Indian as a Prisoner, to see if he belonged to the same band as killed our Bretheren[.] when the Wagon stoped at the schoolhouse to put the prisiner in, there was 2 other Indians in the street which belonged to another Band[.] he wanted to go off with them, and run away to make the atempt, but was stoped and placed underguard[.] I was helping to guard him[.] one of the other Indians went off and told his story to his band and they soon came whoping and yelling down through the street to the school house thinking to scare us off[.] they no doubt intended to make trouble but finding every man prepared for them it cooled them down[.] they then said they now was not mad but wanted to be freindly, I was standing in the door way as they road up[,] and did not realize the danger that there was[.] the Indian Prisoner tried to push past me but I pushed him back into the room[.] Brother Maughan had a long talk with them through an interpreter[.] they promised to go and hunt up the ones that done the killing[.] this excitement broke up our celebration

The affair with the Indians made it necessary to guard the stock almost continually, but by the end of July most of the Indians had left the settlement. Some of the remaining ones appeared friendly, and others:

...were mad and would not go to hunt up there murderers as they agreed to[.] We had to be all the time on the look out for them day and night, having to carry our arms with us when we were outside of the settlement in the fields

In spite of the problems they caused, when the Indians later returned asking for an ox, the Saints gave them one.

Tithing, as we know it, was often paid differently in Henry's time.

Sep 15 ...the Bishop called for saw logs to make tithing bins to put the grain in

By the middle of October Henry and his father were making a business trip to Salt Lake City. As usual, Henry was in attendance for Sunday meetings.

(Oct.) 21 Sunday, Orson Hyde spoke of our enemies course toward us as a people, said they would yet plead for us to go back to Jackson County Missori, and would even offer assistance to go back[.] Prest Young followed upon the same subject, he said when this people went back he expected to own enough means to take them back, he said the Lord was able to take care of his own, without the help of the Gentiles

East winds were common in the Salt Lake Valley.

(Nov.) 18 Bro Benson came home from Salt Lake City, and give an account of a very bad wind storm in that valley blowing down and unruffing houses and Barnes, and blowing away hay and straw and every thing moveable

Church socials were also common, but on occasion some members got overly rambunctious.

(Nov.) 30 Some of the Bretheren got up a Dance, and during the evening some acted very disorderly

Dec 2 Sunday, they were called upon to make an acknowledgment for their conduct[.] some did but not all

On December 17 President Maughan asked the people to sign petitions requesting Congress for weekly mail, and for the legislature to grant Cache Valley a full military organization. At the same time they asked for a charter for Logan City—it was to be the county seat.

Even though the very presence of the Saints in Cache Valley was a great sacrifice, they were asked to do much more for the future of the Valley and of the Territory.

(Jan.) 27 Sunday, E.T. Benson, spoke upon the object of Prest Young sending back to the Missouri river next summer about 200 Ox Teams to bring on the poor saints from that point and to save so much ready cash for outlay for teams on the other end of the journey and we was expected to be called upon from this [valley] 20 Teams with 4 yoak of Oxen with teamsters

On February 10, 1861, the call came for the teams.

...the Brethern felt very liberal in making up what would be wanted

Ezra T. Benson had been elected a member of the legislature and had returned from a session. A party was given in his honor and some of the same shenanigans that occurred at the last party occurred again.

(Feb.) 13 A party was gotten up in honor of Bro Benson arrival from the Legeslature, it was a good party inside, but some disgraceful work on the outside by some drunken fools, carried on

(Feb.) 17 Sunday, the Drunkards was brought up to give an account of themselves, and result was four of them was cut off the church for their unchristian like conduct Namly [Names in original journal] and some other was strongly reproved

A week later, Henry also noted that Brother (name in original journal) was brought to task over a misunderstanding between him and his elders quorum president.

On that same Sunday they were asked to donate funds for the construction of a new meetinghouse. Up to this time church meetings had been held under the bower or in the schoolhouse.

Mar 3 Sunday the report of subscriptions[1] was given in, it amounted to nearly $15,000

---

[1] An agreement to pay a certain amount of money, periodically, toward the meetinghouse.

The earlier call for oxen was now no longer just a call. Between March 17, and April 10, five teamsters[1] were picked from Logan. They included John B. Thatcher, Charles C. Cowley, Harvey C. Dilly, Elisha H. Rogers and David W. Davidson.

Oxen had been wintered north of the Great Salt Lake. Probably they were on, or just east of, Promontory Point. A group of men was dispatched to bring them in and form them into teams. Thomas E. Ricks picked the teams from the best of the donated oxen; one of Henry's animals was chosen.

On April 10 the Logan teamsters were camped and waiting at the church house for the other teams and teamsters from the surrounding settlements before making their departure.

The Church in Logan was really growing now. It had become necessary to divide Logan into wards.

(Apr.) 14   The Ward was devided into 4 Wards with a President or acting Bishop over each Ward[.] Benjamin M [Last name torn from journal, but it was Lewis] for the first ward, myself over the Second Ward[,] John B Thatcher over the Third Ward and Thomas X Smith over the Fourth Ward

Henry was just a few months past twenty-nine when this call came, and he describes one of his duties in this new calling.

(Apr.) 30   A large number of Indians came into Logan from the north feeling very freindly but hungery[.] the Bishop[2] called up the Bishops of the various wards to collect some provisions for them which was done

---

[1] Teamsters in Henry's time drove wagons. Teamsters today usually drive trucks.

[2] This is a reference to Bishop Preston who was once Bishop of all of Logan. Logan had not been organized into stakes yet, and Bishop Preston seemed to be the presiding bishop.

On May 2 Henry ended his first two years in the Valley by the

> ...rebaptizing of those who needed it in their several Wards, 3 of those had been lately cut off namely [Names in original journal] was Baptized into the church

Indians, wagons, and weather did occupy a great deal of Henry's time. They dictated his lifestyle to a great degree.

Now a new event was in store for him—one that would change his life forever.

THE BISHOP
AND MARGARET

Chapter Seven

It was May of 1861, but Henry's journal entry of October 20, 1859, is worth repeating. It is actually the very beginning of the aforementioned event.

> Started a little after sunrise, and as we come to the hub of the road, one coming from north Ogden and the other across the bottoms, we met Bro Thomas McNeil and famiely who had just come across the plains and was going to Cache to hunt him a home[.] he was pleased to learn we were going to that place, and we was equaly pleased of the company,...

Margaret,[1] the oldest daughter of Thomas McNeil, remembers the meeting this way:

> When we had a sufficient supply of food we left Ogden and had not gone far when we met Henry Ballard and Aaron Dewitt who had been to conference and were returning to their homes in Cache Valley. This was my first meeting with my husband. At the time of this meeting I was a barefooted, sun-burned little girl, driving my cow along the dusty country road, but it was impressed on my mother and to my husband at that time that I would some day be his wife. Brother

---

[1] Her autobiography will be quoted or referred to on occasion. A slightly abbreviated autobiography can be found as an appendix to this work.

Ballard and Aaron Dewitt helped us greatly during our journey as we traveled together to Cache Valley....

Margaret had been fifteen for only a month when Henry penned this entry into his journal:

(May) 5 I was married by Bishop Wm B Preston to Margaret Reid McNeil, Daughter of Thomas and Jennet Reid McNeil[.] she was Born April 14, 1846 in Tranent Haddingtonshire Scotland

Later in life, Margaret tells of her courtship with Henry.

I had been keeping company with Brother Ballard for some time, and although I was but fifteen years old, he wanted to marry me. He felt that he could provide for me and take better care of me and save me from working so hard. Brother Ballard went to my father and asked for his consent to my marriage and much to his surprise my father objected, saying that he had to have my help for some time. How much does she earn? Brother Ballard asked. Five dollars a month, was the reply. So it was agreed between the two that Brother Ballard would pay my father $5.00 a month for two years if he would consent to our marriage[1]

If a honeymoon took place, it must have been a short one, for two days later Henry notes:

(May) 17 I helped with about 20 teams to put in Bishop Prestons Wheat into the ground

The balance of the month was spent in doing routine things and helping make his parents' move from Salt Lake City to Logan complete and permanent.

(May) 31 Bro James Cragun came up from Mill Creek to b[u]y my fathers place which he left down there

The month of June passed without comment from Henry, but some July entries are rather interesting.

The Church faced problems during that time which are still common in a more modern age.

---

[1] This version is not found in Margaret's autobiography. It was taken from notes of family members, and is attributed to Margaret.

> July 6 I attented the High council meeting and the Bishop of
> Richmond was droped for carelessness

Indians, still abundant in Cache valley, continued to be a concern to the Saints:

> (July) 12 About 1500 Indians came into the south end of the
> valley very hungry but not unfreindly

> (July) 13 They came into the city and we collected some
> flour for them and they went away very freindly[.] the next
> day 1300 lbs more flour was give to them

Friendly they may have been, still, the Saints felt they bore watching.

> (July) 15 The minute men was called out to watch their
> movements[.] also the foot men was ordered to be in
> readiness[,] also praded some about[.] this time we was also
> troubled with theives so we had to be on the look out day and
> night

> July 24 A meeting was called showing us our position with
> the Indians camped so near to us and some days not more
> than 6 or 8 men in the city[.] he[1] advised us to arange for
> each Ward to stay at home in turn

Indians stayed in the general area, but caused only minor problems. Henry started cutting a good crop of grain at the end of July. In August he was called to join the minuteman company.

> Sep 1 I was called upon with other Brethern to go to some of
> the south settlements[.] we went to Providence where the
> Indians were camped and was doing more or less damage by
> letting their horses into the grain feilds

> (Sept.) 8 I went around my Ward and gathered up some
> Melons and took them to the Indian [camp]

The welfare of the Saints, regarding the Indians, never seemed to leave anyone's mind. President Young, D. H.

---

[1] There is no mention as to who "he" is. It was likely Bishop
Preston, or a militia leader. At that time, the militia leaders were
generally Church-appointed leaders.

Wells, and George Albert Smith arrived from Salt Lake City to meet with the Saints. Their talks revolved around the Indians and how the Saints should protect themselves from them.

(Sept.) 10 ...Prest Young said it was not every one that knew how to handle a gun, he never rested upon the mussle [muzzle] of it...[He] counciled the people to feed the Indians and not fight them

(Sept.) 18   General C. W. West and his staff from Ogden came to view the troops of the valley and inspect their arms...

(Sept.) 20 We held a grand Reveiw of Arms[.] commenced at 10 A.M. and kept it up till evening...

Ever faithful to his journal, Henry records things both ordinary and not so ordinary. The spectrum is broad.

(Sept.) 23   We held the first Agricutureal fair in the valley

(Sept. 24)   Sunday, Bros Benson and Maughan spoke upon the necesity of us building a meeting house for our present use, till we could build our Tabernacle,[1] and that we build it 30–54 ft[.] and each ward to get up a subscription list, and teams to start the coming week to get out the timbers for it[.] The Bishop called upon me to go and take charge of the Boys getting the timber out[.] I took 2 yoak of oxen and provisions to last a week[.] I drove the first log down the mountain for our Logan hall, we done [it] till it stormed

(Sept.)   I was helping to raise the roof of our new Hall[.] Bishop Preston give us some of the contents of a letter from Bro Benson, stating that the Prest [President] of the U.S. had demanded our quota of men for the northern army, as they were ingaged in a civil war between the north and south, although we were only a Teritory[.] yet if we did not comply we were threatened, but we knew they could not compel us; The Bishop gave the privilage for each ward to have a dance in the old schoolhouse on differant nights

(Sept.) 26   The first Ward had theirs

---

[1] What Henry refers to as the tabernacle was really the Logan Hall. The Logan Tabernacle came quite a few years later.

(Sept.) 27 The second Ward commenced theirs but it was a very dark wet night and the roof of the schoolhouse leaked so bad we had to breake it up and wait for another opportunity

(Sept.) 29 Bros Benson and C. W. West came up from the City to hold mass meetings in every settlement to elect deligates to a convention in S. L. City to get up a State Organization and to send deligates to congress to be admitted as a state in the Union

(Sept.) 30 A mass meeting was held and the business attended to with a harty response[.] the 3rd ward held their party[.] I was taken very sick with a cold and sore throat[.] it was raining nearly every day and had been for nearly two months

(Oct.) 3 It stormed so bad covering everything up with snow—

(Oct.) 4 Storming again snowing all over the valley

(Oct.) 7 We returned to the canyon again

(Oct.) 8 It commenced snowing again about noon falling very fast and cold[.] with it we had to go home again

(Oct.) 18 I started to Salt Lake City, I took my Wife and mother with me[.] We staid at Wellsville at Bro Wm Poppletons

(Oct,) 21 We reached the city...

(Oct.) 26 My wife Margaret received her endowments[.] was sealed to me the same day

(Oct.) 27 Went to the Tabernacle[.] Prest Young spoke upon the necesity of us producing every thing we needed

(Oct.) 28 We started back home and arrived on the 31st

(Nov 5 I again went to the canyon for more timber

(Nov.) 11 Helping to fit up a team to haul corn for the team [that is] going to haul rock for the Temple in Salt Lake City

Jany 1 [1862] The fourth ward held their party

(Jan.) 7 The second Ward had their party...

(Jan.) 16 I got my grain thrashed[.] it was not so very wet considering so much rain that we had had during the winter

(Jan.) 29 A meeting was called and Prest Maughan give us some of the doings at the convention[.] said that Prest Young felt well and said the time had come for this people to assert their rights and it was the will of the Lord that they should do so[.] Next came that the Indians had killed some cattle at our own herd and some more brethern was sent out to the herd

The entries dating back to September 23, 1861, cover a period of about four months. Some significant things took place during that time: the first fair, an effort to involve the people in gaining statehood, involvement in the construction of the Salt Lake Temple, and the beginning of the first Logan church house. Of equal importance: Margaret received her endowments and was sealed to Henry. The everpresent problem with the Indians remained the same.

Through Henry's words it is easy to gain an appreciation for the great efforts made in spite of the adverse circumstances under which the Saints were living.

Splinter groups came into being almost as soon as the Church was organized. Henry still mentions them in 1862.

Feby 1   The high council met in the Tithing office and droped John E. Jones[,] one of their number[,] for apostasey[.] he had joined the Morrisites[.] one Joseph Morris had arrisen [from] the Weber claiming to have revelations[.] he was getting quite a number to follow him

The quest for self-sufficiency among the members of the Church is a well-known goal. The General Authorities brought it up in Henry's day just as they do now.

(Feb.) 16   Our new Hall was opened and Dedicated, a letter was read from Prest Young showing the necesity of sending to the states for machinery for home manufactory[.] some machines was donated for that purpose

(Feb.) 23   Bro Benson preposed that we open the Logan Canyon and A committee was appointed to explore...

Mar 1   A council was called to consider the best plan to have a road built[.] it was decided to take shares of stock and the shares to be $25.00 and toal to be 50 cts [per] person

Mar 2   The plan of opening the road was accepted and shares were taken[.] a letter was read from Prest Young stating that 300 teams would be sent back this summer for the poor and 30 was the quota for Cache valley

Imagine—300 teams and wagons, loaded with provisions and volunteer drivers, to drive all the way back to the Missouri River. A journey of more than 2,000 miles that would consume months of precious time. Most of the drivers were asked to leave a family at home to be cared for by others, or to sustain themselves.

(Mar.) 3   A general election of officers for the state of Deseret and the constitution was accepted

(Mar.) 16   The teamsters for Logan was called[,] 7 of them[,] namely [:] Barney Stanford, Wm Ricks, Sidney Dibble, J Denning, Morgan Evans, Fredric Goodwin, and Robert Roberts[.] the Bretheren all responded

(Mar.) 30   Bro Benson counciled the Bretheren to hold on to their bread stuff and not let the gentiles have it, as there was expected a great imigration to Salmon river as gold had been discovered there, it was about 200 miles north of us, then in Washington Teritory

April 28   The teams started for S. L. City to go to Florence on the Missori river

(Apr.) 30   I commenced putting my crop in, the ground was very wet

(May) 16   We had a fine rain which done a great deal of good as the land was getting very dry

May of 1862 also brings to an end the first year of married life for the bishop and Margaret.

Margaret McNeil Ballard,
first wife of Henry Ballard

THE
EARLY 1860S

Chapter Eight

The early 1860s, in Cache Valley, were filled with hardship.

> June 15 [1862] Sunday a cloud burst on the mountains between Logan and Green Canyon coming down both canyons and washing out the roads and bridges that we had just built[.] a washing out the road in green canyon and washing lots of gravel down onto the farms below, the streams was very high all over the Teritory washing away nearly all the Bridges, it was said to be the highest waters ever known in the settlement of Utah

> (June) 18 We turned and worked upon the road in green canyon til we got it so we could use it again

Again the splinter group, the Morrisites, is mentioned.

> (June) 22 An account came in the Deseret News about the Band of Morrisites, they had been imprisoning some of thier men for wanting to leave their camp, and the freinds of the imprisoned entered a complaint to cheif Justice Hinney, whereupon he issued a writ of Habeus Corpus, Directing Morris to liberate the prisoners and give them a fair trial before his honor but they refused and threatened the officers that served the writ, the Judge then Issued another writ and sent a posse of 200 men to serve it and to take Morris and his leaders to S. L. City to be tried for false imprisonment, but they resisted and mustered their men about 100 armed[,] and commenced firing into the posse and killed 2 of their number,

59

Smith and Wahler[.] they kept up their position for 3 days before they would surrender, and during this time Joseph Morris and John [Bank] were killed, the posse took 3 of their other leaders and nintey of others to S. L. City for examination and they were bound...

Henry says little about July 1862, but does mention he helped "fit up the Bowery" for the Fourth of July. They fired guns and had a parade and speeches, followed by a theater group in the evening. The bowery was so crowded the show ran for two nights.

The Pioneer Days celebration seemed more significant to Henry, for he notes:

(July) 24 We killed a beef and 4 sheep in each ward and give to the people to eat at their own homes, we had a good meeting after our long procession with the pioneers, Mormon battalion, and 24 Silver Grays, 24 Mothers in Israel, 24 Young men, and 24 young Ladies, and 24 little Boys, and 24 Girls[.] we had a good time

Little is said of August. September is not so silent. He mentions an early frost "which cut the vines and corn."

September 12 found him in bed with a cold and sore throat. He was administered to by his father and his father-in-law and recovered quickly.

(Sept) 15 I commenced hauling my wheat again

To the Saints the problem of Indians must have seemed an eternal one.

(Sept) 23 We had to again move our young stock and guard them again against the Indians as they were already on horses

(Sept) 28 News came at noon that the Indians had stole a band of horses from the church farm, owned mostly by Thatchers[.] the Horse men that had horses up just [jumped] into their saddles and was soon after them[.] we joined them along the foot of the mountains until we got to Franklin, when they took through the mountain[.] we still followed them bearing east toward Bear Lake[.] 4 of the boys came onto them a little before dark, when the Indians run into the Brush ready to fight, and the boys returned to meet the rest of us, but before we got up they had run on again with the Horses, and it got so dark we had to camp for the night

(Sept) 29   We started again at day light and Picked up some horses that had given out while they were rushing them so fast, we sent 5 of the boys back with these horses, and then followed them through very thick timber till we deemed it not wise to follow them any farther into this thick timber as we had none come close unto them and was now in a basin where we had no chance to take advantage of them but they had every advantage of us, we was also out of Provisions and our horses were given out

Oct 1   News came that the Indians was collecting near Franklin intending to make trouble[.] 25 horse men was sent to look after them

(Oct) 5   We were all called out that had horses to go to Franklin[.] we went and returned the same night

Other things needed to be accomplished along with chasing Indians—things that required a great deal of effort, such as raising and harvesting grain. Grain was needed for barter because cash was so hard to come by. Then, as now, efforts were often made in vain.

(Oct) 6   I started with my wife to S. L. City, we went to Willard City and staid at Bro Wm Brewertons

(Oct) 10   We got through with our business, not being able to trade off our grain for clothing[.] we returned[.] went to Farmington and staid with Robt Camm

They must have needed clothing badly to consider sitting in a wagon for nearly a week in the cool, if not cold, October air. No hint of anger or even disappointment is evident in Henry's journal. This is a lesson in patience and restraint.

President Young traveled to Logan on occasion to instruct the Saints in a variety of things.

(Oct.) 21   I was gathering up oats to feed Prest [Presidents] company horses[.] they came in at sundown all feeling well

(Oct.) 22, [1862]   The meeting commenced in the Hall but not for more than half the people assembled[.] Prest Young spoke upon classification of labor[.] the rest of the Bretheren that spoke followed in the same strain of remarks....The Prest held another meeting the next day and returned home...

An earlier entry noted that the Saints from Cache Valley were asked to furnish wagons and drivers to help immigrants come West.

Henry's last entry continues:

...our teams commenced to arrive from the east, they took more cattle than before[,] averageing one Ox to each team[.] they left one of my fathers oxen in the mountains, Father and myself started after it the next day,...we hunted in the mountains that evening but could not find it[.] Father staid at the herd house and I went on to Willard

Octr 24,   I started back about noon, the Prest had got into Brigham City and the flags was flying as I passed it[.] I overtook my father in Wellsville canyon[.] he had found the Ox, we got it to Wellsville and staid there that night

(Oct.) 25   We got it home but badly used up

Henry's journal speaks for itself for the next year or so. The subjects are of such a variety it is difficult to categorize them. Equally difficult is the process of elimination. Nearly every entry has historical or religious significance, or supplies us with an insight concerning Henry and the lives of his contemporaries. It seems prudent, therefore, to record them in his words with little or no comment.

(Nov.) 23   Some of Col Connors command came to Logan to get a white boy from the Indians that they took from an emigrant train some where out north a few years ago, the Indians learned of their coming and took to the mountains, the Soilders chased one and caught him[.] they afterward caught some more and they then went to fetch the boy

(Nov. 24)   They brought the boy into camp

1862 Nov. 25   The Soilders started back to the city, and the Indians came out of the mountains hungery and begging[.] we had to feed them instead of the Soilders, we collected Bread and Beef for them, they then went away feeling well

Dec 4 (1862) Bro's Benson, Maughan and Preston Started to the Legeslature

(Dec.) 10 We had our first snow in the valley for the season

(Dec.) 21 A donation of meat was taken up for the hands working the S. L. City Temple

Jany 7 [1863] The Indians killed an emigrant north of Franklin, he was coming into this valley in company with 8 others to get provisions to take out to the Salmon river Gold mines

(Jan.) 18 My wife Margaret Brought me a little girl about 12 midnight, we named her after her mother and my mother, namely (Margaret Hannah)

(Jan.) 24 Bro's Benson & Maughan came home

(Jan.) 25 Sunday, they give us the account of their work at the Legeslature,...Govenor Harding would not sign any of the bills that they had passed by both houses, it looked like their time had been a failure

Jany 27 Col Connor came into Mendon with about 450 Troops on the road north, above Franklin to hunt the Indians that had been killing emigrants about Salmon river

(Jan.) 28 They passed through Logan a little before daylight making it their buisness to travel by night so that the Indians could not see them on the road

(Jan.) 29 They got to Franklin and went on over Bear river, and surprised the Indians and commenced fighting them, and kept it up for 3 or 4 hours with a loss of 15 Soilders killed and 40 wounded, and about 200 Indians killed and 150 ponies taken from them, this put a quietous upon the Indians, the Lord raised up this foe to punish them without us having to do it[.] we had bore a great deal from them and still had been feeding them, yet some of the wicked spirits amongst them would stir up trouble against us[1]

---

[1] This incident was the Bear River Massacre. It occurred twelve miles north of Franklin, Idaho. See Bancroft, vol. 26, pp. 631–32.

(Jan.) 31 They returned and camped in the Tithing yard over night[.] A number of them got their feet badly frozen, they took their dead and wounded back to the City with them

Feby 1, (1863 They left Logan with their booty of Ponies

(Mar,) 1 (1863) Prest Manuhan got a letter from S.L. City stateing that 500 teams would be wanted to go back to Florence again for the poor saints coming to Utah and it was expected they would leave S.L. City about the 25 of April and the quota for Cache valley would be 53 with their full fitout...

(Mar.) 8 ...Bro Benson came back from the City, and enformed us that our great Govenor Harding had been trying to make trouble for this people, and the Citizians of S. L. City held a mass meeting and they resolved to have him removed and to have good men as Govenors and Judges or not at all,...

April 10 (1863) The ground was covered with 6 inches of snow in places [.] in S. L.valley it had fallen a foot deep

April 12 (1863) Sunday the Bretheren give us the news of the conference[.] it was gathering the poor, Building the Temple, also Building a large Tabernacle in the City, 250 by 150 ft claculated to seat 1200 people and a missionary fund to send the missionaries to their feilds of labor and support their famielies while they were gone, and we was to haul the Tithing wheat to S. L. City this summer

May 1 (1863) News came that a Bro had been shot by the Indians at Franklin wounding him very badly, they were stealing horses all the time

(May) 9 Some of the horse company was called to go to Paradise in the South end of the valley, the Indians had been stealing horses and cattle around there, and the Brethern had taken a few of them prisoners, again news came in the evening that they had driven off all the Horses and Cattle in the little valley[1] belonging to Brigham City, in open day also killed a man in the mountains who was burning charcoal...

---

[1] The little valley Henry refers to is probably the valley east of Brigham City where Mantua is now located.

(May) 11 Bro's Benson & Maughan went to Paradise and had a talk with the Indians, they let the prisoners go with a promise that they would bring the horses back

June 9 (1863) I started to S. L. City with my horse team with a load of Tithing Wheat

(June) 14 I returned home, a large emigration was coming into S. L. City from the states going to the Salmon river mines, also to California to get away from the cival war that was going on in the states between the north and the south

(July) 24 While the Bretheren was fireing a salute upon the anvil, it Burst, and Badly injured Bro's Thos Lockyer who was fireing it, also Bro Joseph E. Hyde who was standing near by

Sep 13 (1863) Our teams returned home from Florence

Dec 6 (1863) Bro Musser preached to us on the necesity of paying our Tithing and fulfilling all our oblegations that we may be Blest

(Dec.) 17 I went around the ward and gathered up some old clothing for James Thomas and famiely which was in distress through getting their clothing burnt...

(Dec.) 20 I got a letter from Box Elder telling the where abouts of my Fathers Oxen that was lost last fall[.] Going to S. L. City with Tithing wheat

(Dec.) 28 Bro's Maughan and Preston came home for the hollidays[.] also a special message from Prest Young to stop the selling of any more wheat to the Salmon river and Bannock City miners, as all the surplus was needed in the City[.] Prest Young was paying $3.00 per Bushel in cash for all he could get, for the Calafornia volunteers was out of Bread, and they had called upon the church to furnish them[.] in the evening the Second ward party came off, we had a good time

(Dec.) 31 The Presidents request was brought before the people and they all responded to it

(Jan.) 6 It was a very cold day and we had 3 of the coldest since Dec. 2 1858 when several men was frozen to death

(Jan.) 17 Sunday some home missionaries came to Logan from S. L. City sent by Prest Young to preach throughout the valley to awaken an intrest among the people in regard to their duties[.] Bro Joseph W. Young spoke at some length also

Hector C Haight and Bro Shipp[.] in the evening Brigham Young Jr. Spoke upon the virtues of this people and the plans of our enemies to come out here in the Spring by the tens of thousands to search these mountains for gold mines in order to over run us in our elections and lead the young in paths of vice,...

Jany 31 ...Bro Benson was called on a mission to the Sandwich Islands[1] to go and straiten things up there

Feby 21 (1864) Bro's Musser and Sheets from S. L. City came with a message from Prest Young asking the people here to sell him all the surplus wheat for S. L. City at $2.00 per bushel at our doors for the poor of that City needed it

(Feb.) 28 The teams were again called to gather the poor[.] 300 was called for this season and 30 of that number from Cache Valley and 6 from Logan[.] mules and horse teams were called for this season as well as Ox teams[.] Wm B Preston was again called as captain of the company going from this and ajoining vallies...the teamsters of Logan was called[:] John A. Cowley, Hans Munk, Hans Peterson, and myself as Ox teamsters and Edward Nelson and James Goodwin mule Teamsters

This might sound like a grand adventure for Henry, but consider the following circumstances: Margaret, his wife, was only eighteen years old, and the mother of a new daughter, Margaret Hannah. In addition, she was expecting a second child. Henry was not a wealthy person and this call would tax his limited means, and he was still bishop of the Second Ward. Who would act as bishop in his absence? Henry didn't even have a counselor or ward clerk. Still he never questioned the calling—he just did the best he could.

Now a trek—one that would test the mettle of many men, including Henry—was about to begin.

---

[1] The Sandwich Islands are known now as the Hawaiian Islands.

EAST FOR
EMIGRANTS

Chapter Nine

On March 21, 1864, Henry noted:

I commenced plowing

It was important to him to plow and plant crops even though he would not be home to harvest them. His wife would need all the income and food she could get to survive in his absence. Arrangements for Margaret were made, but the time for departure was quickly arriving and many other details needed to be addressed as well.

(Mar) 28 A general training day for both Cavalry and foot[.] there was a big turn out. A letter was read from General D. H. Wells to be fully organized with baggage wagons and every thing ready to go to any part day or night[1]

1864 April 15 I was helping to fit up our teams in readiness to start

(Apr.) 16 We started out this time to Wyhoming[.] we took loads of Tithing wheat to S. L. City[.] we camped at Wellsville

---

[1] Henry does not mention whether the training pertained to the trip east or to something local. He says "to any part day or night." It sounds more like any part of the Valley.

(Apr.) 17 We went to the Big Springs Between Wellsville and Mendon and waited there for our captain W B Preston[.] we had to go around the mountain by Mendon on account of the bad roads[1]

Many future entries list names of places where they camped. Little else is said, although he mentions that on April 22 no cattle food was available, and so he stood guard all night to keep the stock from wandering away in search of something to eat. He also notes the party's arrival in Salt Lake City.

(Apr.) 23 ...and unloaded our tithing wheat and went 4 miles up Emigration Canyon and camped

The route taken would have been the same route followed by Saints for years, but it is interesting to mention some of the places they camped for the night. Names like Barnards Springs, Ogden Bottoms, Sessions Settlement, Parleys Park, and Silver Creek provoke a note of interest. All were along the Wasatch Front. Further east was Sulfer Creek, Grass Creek, Little Sandy, Big Sandy, Dry Sandy, The Muddy, Dear Creek, Boise Creek, Pacific Springs, Allocolic Creek, and Laperlay.

Also mentioned were Labontay, Horse Shoe Creek, Horse Creek, Ash Hollow, Bakers Ranch, and Fremont Slough. There was Plumb Creek, Hopeville, Kerney Post, Beaver Creek, Big Blue, Salt Creek, Minneaha Creek, and Weeping Water.[2]

Many of the names are gone now, as are the pioneers who designated them. These places were the unwritten

---

[1] The bad roads would be in either Sardine Canyon or Wellsville Canyon, the present highway. Around the mountain meant going north to what is now called the Valley View Highway. It went through Beaver Dam and Collinston and would take them an extra day of travel.

[2] The spellings are Henry's. Allocolic was probably Alcoholic. Dear Creek was probably Deer Creek, etc.

signposts of the prairie, and they were as necessary to our forefathers as convenience stops are to us, one hundred fifty years later. Grass and water were their fuel.

The dullness of plodding alongside or sitting behind the oxen, day after day, was oftentimes punctuated with less mundane happenings. Consider the following and its implications:

(Apr.) 27 ...we had to leave Bro A. Thorn sick with a famiely, he was badly afflicted with Rehmatic

The likelihood of Brother Thorn being taken in by anyone but strangers seems improbable. When he recovered he would again be at the mercy of strangers. He would need help to find his way home or to catch up with the wagon train going to the East.

Organization has always been of paramount importance to the Church. This trip was no exception.

(Apr.) 28 We came up with the other part of our company who was from Box Elder County[,] also Weber County[.] they came up through Weber Canyon[.] Here we made a full organization by appointing a chaplain[,] five captains of ten and four Night horse guards[,] two to be on duty at a time

Henry continues:

(May) 17 While we where yoaking up our cattle in the Morning Albert Baker the assistant captain rode fast on the outside of the corral of wagons and the ground sounded like it was hollow[.] the noise excited the cattle and they made a rush for the opposite end of the corral and started off at full gallop[.] they knocked down 3 men and some oxen and upset one wagon but did not do much harm, after we got started and was passing Independance rock, the excited cattle again started to run but one soon got them stoped, we nooned on Grease wood creek and camped on the South fork of the same

(May) 18 We traveled all day without water till we struck the North Platte where we camped by the side of a large emigrant camp going to the northern mines[.] old

Captain Bridger[1] (of fort Bridger) was piloting them over a new road, with about 100 wagons

(May) 19 (1864) Traveled down the river to the upper bridge expecting to cross it, but they wanted to charge us $3.00 per Wagon to cross it, We went Seven miles farther down and got the chance of crossing this Bridge for fifty cents per wagon

(May) 20 We crossed the Platte at this Bridge onto the South side and here traded for some Buffloo robes of a mountaineer and camped five miles below

(June) 4 Went up Ash Hollow going South over to the South Platte 18 miles and nooned, here we found the river booming high, and no way to cross it only having to ford and swim it, a number of the Bretheren that could swim went into the river to hunt a ford, they finally concluded that 2 miles above the old Calafornia crossing was the best place, at the Buckeye ranch the river was three forth of a mile whide, we commenced to cross at 4 p.m[.] in some places the cattle would have to swim[,] then they could ford it while the wagons would float[.] we had to wade it holding onto our oxen when we come to the deep channels, after we had got about half way over some of the teams had got down too low coming too near to some of the islands, in one of these places five Wagon Boxes floated off[2][.] we got them out the best we could, we succeeded in getting four out that night

(June) 5 (1864) When we went to get the other one out we found that [a] burr[3] had worked off and the wheel was gone

---

[1] "Old Captain Bridger," as Henry calls him, is the same Jim Bridger of Cache Valley fame. He had trapped the Valley some thirty or forty years earlier. He once followed the Bear River down to the Great Salt Lake, tasted the water, found it salty, and declared it must be an arm of the Pacific Ocean.

[2] The boxes were not fastened to the wagons, and in deep water would float like a boat. They sat between the wagon bolsters so it would be convenient to exchange wagon boxes when necessary.

[3] A burr is a threaded nut used to hold the wagon wheel on the wagon axle. They are square and about two inches across. Wheels were often removed to apply axle grease, and the nuts would often work loose.

and burried up in some hole and we could not find the wheel any whare and we had to give it up[.] we got the wagon out and took it to peices and loaded it up in other wagons and got a new wheel when we got to the Missori river, we lost a few things[.] we was meeting about 200 Teams per day going to the new Gold fields in the north, many taking their famielies with them to get away from the war[1] that was still rageing[.] we went 15 miles and camped at the lone tree ranch

(June) 12 Went 8 miles and nooned, here we left 59 head of our weakest cattle to recrute[2] up at a ranch till we returned...

(June) 14 Went 25 miles and camped

(June) 15 Nooned, 11 miles below at the junction of the road where it leaves the river 40 miles below Kerney, we took the road leaving the river which lead toward Nebraska City[.] we went 10 miles further and camped at some springs, where the captains and guards Horses run away, but the camp guard soon got them back

(June) 21 Went within 4 miles of Wyoming[3][,] the landing place for the Saints this season

Wyoming, Nebraska, must have been their destination. It took from April 16 until June 21, a total of about 65 event-filled days to get there. The next several entries describe their scurrying to and fro in hurried preparation for the return trip.

1864 June 22, Some of the Brethern went to see the emigrants, about 100 had arrived, the captain went in to get his Instructions from Joseph W. Young who had charge of this seasons emigration.

---

[1] Reference is made to the Civil War.

[2] One meaning of recruit is: to renew or restore back to health again. It was commonly used in Henry's day.

[3] Do not confuse this Wyoming with the state of the same name. Henry's journal confirms the fact that a Wyoming existed near Nebraska City.

(June) 23 (1864)   I went to Nebraska City to get some Blacksmithing done, and to trade a little, but everything was very high on account of the war that was going on.

(June) 24   I went to Wyoming and staid over night

(June) 25   Was helping to fix up some new wagons and makeing arrangements to get me a cook stove hauled through which I done.[1]

(June) 28   We moved our Wagons to Wyoming and sent the most of our cattle back to the old camp[.] we then commenced to load up our Wagons

(June) 29-30   Still loading up

(July) 1 (1864) I went to Nebraska City after a wagon

(July) 3   800 more emigrants arrived at Wyoming[.] all the Utah trains had arrived

(July) 4   We moved 4 miles out this time taking Platte road,[2] we was very heavy loaded, we had 380 passengers and their baggage and Provisions and 1500 lbs of Freight to each of the 50 wagons.

(July) 5   I unloaded my 40 sacks of flour giving one to each wagon and returned for a load of grociers[.] I then took this load to camp and devided up amongst the Passengers to last them to Laramie

(July) 6   I then went back for my load of grociers to take across the plains, the reason that I did not have any passengers was that I had been cooking for the captain all the way down and we had slept together in going down, and he wanted me to still cook for him and the Logan Boys[,] 8 of us together, so I had my wagon more to myself but it filled to the top[.] I could hardly find a corner to lay down, the captain slept with Hans Munk upon a load of flour where there was more room

(July) 7-8   The clerks was settling up with the emigrants

---

[1] "Hauled through" probably means Henry bought a new cook stove for Margaret, or someone else, and was hauling it through to Cache Valley.

[2] This "4 miles" appears to be a gathering place rather than an actual start west, for there was still unfinished business to attend to.

(July) 9   They finished up with them and we moved 4 miles[.][1]

The journey back to Utah had now begun. It was midsummer—mostly hot and dusty. They knew the trail, so other than heat, the trip should have been routine. But was it?

(July) 11 Made one drive[.] we had a very heavy rain

(July) 15 A Woman and child died in camp

(July) 16 (1864) We buried them 6 miles below where the road come down onto the Platte Bottom

1864 July 19 A woman died in camp 60 years of age

(July) 22 A son was born in camp,...

(July) 24 Another child died in camp,...

(July) 26 We came up to our cattle at noon where we left them going down[.] they had done well,...

(July) 28 We Traveled 23 miles

(July) 29 Another woman died in camp, we camped 17 miles below Cottonwoods Military post

(July) 31 It was a very hot dusty day[.] we only traveled 15 miles and camped on Fremont Slough

(Aug.) 2 A man Passenger died in camp

(Aug.) 5 Another son was born in camp, we traveled through some very heavy sand...

(Aug.) 6 We crossed the river at Julesburg[2] very well by doubling teams, the water struck the Box in one place...

The Lord giveth and the Lord taketh away. A period of less than twenty days had passed and six people had died. For the surviving family members there was but one choice: leave loved ones in a shallow grave and move on. Death and hardship were not strangers to the Saints.

---

[1] This is likely the same four miles mentioned on his July 4 entry, and probably marked the time when they actually began the westward trek back.

[2] Julesburg is in the northeast corner of present day Colorado.

(Aug.) 7 (1864) Sunday we remained in camp the forepart of
the day to let our cattle rest[.] At noon as we were yoaking up
our oxen, a mule from a little camp near us which had been
traveling with us for protection, this mule had been snake bit
a few days before, he came to the corrall and jumped over
the chain that had been fastened from one wagon wheel to
the other to keep the cattle in, as soon as it jumped it give a
big groan and died[.] this frightened the cattle and they made
a rush to get out of the corrall, they tiped over one wagon and
broke an axle tree and a tounge[.] this was about all the harm
done[.] we had to stop the rest of the day to fix up our
Wagons,...

1864 Aug. 8 We traveled 18 miles[.] in the afternoon as we
were traveling the fore part of the train got to running away
but the Bretheren was luckey in some getting them stopped[.]
the hinder part of our train was behind a devide so we did not
see it nor our cattle partake of the spirit

(Aug.) 9 We traveled 10 miles and nooned by the side of a
large freight Train[1] that had been up to Laramie, and in
coming back had lost 75 head of their cattle out of 600[,] in 8
days[,] by Bloody Murrin,[2][.] and some trains going to Utah
with freight had to leave a portion of their loading at Laramie
on account of their loss of stock, and we had lost several
head and quite a number was sick[.] our Capatin and Reuben
Collett and Warren Childs started back to Julesburg to
Telegraph to Prest Young in S. L. City to get his mind about
going the Pole Creek route, as we beleived it would be better
to go that way as there would be less dust and more feed in
that route[.] we remained in camp that day

(Aug.) 10 We moved camp 5 miles and waited for our
captain and his guard, they came back at dark but he could
not get his dispatch through on account of the Indian
disturbances back on the road[.] The operator would not take
time to send it, so we had to go it on our own account[.] the
Indians had taken a small train of 15 wagons, took their

---

[1] This was a wagon train, not a railroad train. The
transcontinental railway had not been completed by 1864. It is noted
in this same entry that the telegraph lines were intact.

[2] "Bloody Murrin," as Henry called it, is a highly contagious
cattle disease. Today it is known as anthrax. It is usually fatal and
can be transmitted to humans.

stock[,] burnt their wagons, killed the men and took 2 women and 3 children, and run off a large amount of stock about the cotton woods Station. and some other depredations reported[.] the next church train was 60 miles behind us

Time was of the essence to the group. They had left Julesburg August 6, and made the decision to send riders back to Julesburg to wire Brigham Young some time in the afternoon or evening of August 9. If the wagons traveled the usual twenty or so miles each day, they could have been seventy-five miles from the telegraph office. The riders had to travel both ways, and they were still back by the night of August 10—an incredible ride.

Aug 11 Another freight train from Laramie passed us which had lost 50 head of cattle out of 300 in 8 days, and they said another company behind them had lost about the same amount, and the Ranch mens cattle was also dying very fast[.] the captain thought from all the reports that he could gather it would be best to take the Pole Creek[1] route[.] we went on 2 miles to the forks of the road, where it turned off to go to Laramie 40 miles above Julesburg[.] we went on the Pole Creek route trusting in the Lord for our best good

Death still stalked the group. Water was in short supply, or nonexistent in places.

(Aug.) 14 A child died in camp

(Aug.) 15 We crossed the right hand fork of the creek 75 miles from the forks of the road and 115 miles from Julesburg, we traveled the right hand fork[.] We traveled 14 miles without water

1864 Aug 16, We had to camp all night without water[.] it had sunk again for 18 miles[2]

---

[1] It is highly probable that the Pole Creek Henry speaks of is the present-day Lodgepole Creek near Julesburg.

[2] By "sunk," Henry means the water had sunk into the ground. The creek was dry for the next 18 miles.

(Aug.) 17 We started an hour before day light and went 10 miles and stoped for water and rested a while and then traveled on some more

(Aug.) 18 We came over to the head of the left hand fork of Pole Creek and camped at Chyann [Cheyenne] Springs by the ruins of camp Walback 180 miles from Julesburg[.] we had another son born in camp

On August 19, Henry describes "nooning" at "some springs" on Cheyenne Summit while they looked down on a "fine looking valley" with two streams running through it. He describes the "several high mountains around it with everlasting snow on them."

Snow and water may have been visible in the distance, but they traveled sixteen miles the next day without benefit of either.

They watched the mail stage as it turned southward toward Denver. The Pony Express days had come and gone by now.

Noon was spent at aptly named Dry Creek, for it had no water either.

By August 22, they were into rough and rocky country. The wind howled as it blew dust in their faces. Then rain came.

(Aug.) 23 The wind was still blowing very cold but the rain had settled the dust[.] we crossed rock creek and it was well named for it was a very rockey country all over that part[.] we camp up with a company that had went the north Platte road to fort Laramie and when they got to Laramie their cattle commenced dying so fast they thought they would turn back[.] they came over the Pole creek and followed up it[.] in the afternoon we had some very rough places to cross, we got over to the Big Medicine Bowe and camped...

August 25 found them again without water, and on August 26, cattle rustlers became a problem.

1864 Aug 26 Our Cattle was drove up to camp, and it was supposed that some was driven off [judging] by some tracks seen across the river from the herd, we soon yoaked up our cattle and found 5 was missing, the number tracked away, we soon unyoaked again, and the Horse guard and all the Horses in camp that could go, started on their tracks, [they] went and followed them back on the road about 2 miles, and then went down the river, and crossed back onto the same side of the river as they drove them from [it,] and the tracks of 2 horse men following them[.] it had been some men living at the station that had a little hay cut, and they wanted pay for damages and they took that plan to get it[.] after we got them back the captain offered them 2 head of Oxen, but they refused the offer and wanted $500.00 damage for 3 tons of hay as they called it and the captian refused their request[.] they said they would go to fort Halleck and bring on the troops and force their demand upon us[.] we hitched up about 4 p.m. and traveled 16 miles and camped after dark on Sage Creek on very poor feed[.] we put 8 men on guard with the cattle at a time[,] in place of 2 as before

Aug 27 We traveled 10 miles and camped at the pine grove springs station, here we expected to be attacted by the troops if these unjust ranchers could induce them to harken to their story, but no troops appeared

(Aug.) 28 We started at day light and traveled 5 miles and halted for Breakfast, when the camp nearly caught fire, by the sage brush catching fire...

(Aug.) 30 We traveled 15 miles without water...

(Aug.) 31 ...from Green river we went down this creek and camped[.] Another woman died 60 years of age

1864 Sept 4 In the afternoon a heady Thunderstorm over took us and we halted for a short time, and dureing this storm another son was born[.] we passed Rock Springs Station... making 20 miles...

Again, in a matter of five days, the Lord took one and gave one.

Salt Lake City was still several days away—days filled with as much trial as the ones in the past had been.

(Sept) 5 One of the men that had the damages against us at north Platte passed us in the stage going to fort Bridger to try to [get] the troops from there after us, as they had failed to get them from fort Halleck,...nooned at the ford[,] we then forded it...George Langley broke the hind wheel of his wagon all to peices, we loaded up his load into other wagons, then tied a pole under his [axle] and traveled on 3 miles farther[.] we lessoned our guard to 4 at a time

(Sept.) 6 ...we followed up Blacks fork one mile and stoped the remainder of the day and fixed up the Broken wheel

(Sept.) 7 ...we only lost 3 head of Oxen on the Pole Creek route, the Lord greatly favored us by sending great showers of rain ahead of us to fill up the Bitter creek where it so often sunk in ordinary times[,] so we did not suffer much for water for such a big train, and we knew nothing of the road, we saved a great many cattle by coming that way

(Sept.) 9 Two women died of Disintery, we went 20 miles and camped...

(Sept.) 10 We sent 2 men to Bridger to learn what the news was of our percecuters, the Bretheren learned that the commander of the fort would do nothing till he could get orders from Col Conner at camp Douglas Salt Lake City, He sent for an order but got no answer, so our percecuters had to return home without any thing[.] we nooned on the pioneer Ridge[.] After traveling one mile in the afternon we met with a very bad accident [it] happen[ed] to Bro Martin Wood just returning from a mission in England[.] Bro Wood was driving a team at the time loaded with 4000 lbs of Stoves, at noon he fixed up a foot board, but not making it safe, and as he started out he got up to ride with his feet upon the board, and in going down a little incline he lost his balance and the board tipped throwing him in front of the wagon and both near Wheels[1] passed over his neck nearly killing him on the spot, but we took him along a short distance to Sulfer Creek near Bear River[.] we watched over him all night and he felt like he would recover

(Sept.) 11 We left him at Bear River Station and Benjamin Garr with him to help take care of him[.] he appeared a little

---

[1] The near wheels are the two on the driver's side of a wagon. The other two wheels are the far wheels.

better but we learned afterward that he died in 3 days after
we left him,...

(Sept.) 12   I was called to drive this same team after the
accident[.] A child died in camp[.] we camped 2 miles above
the mouth of Echo Canyon

(Sept.) 15   Arrived in Salt Lake City and unloaded our freight
and Passengers that wanted to stop in that part of the country,
the rest we took along to our part of the country[.] we went to
Sessions Settlement

(Sept.) 18   The Logan Brass Band and a number of our
freinds came and met us at Wellsville which cheered us[.] we
camped by the Wellsville feilds

(Sept.) 19   We Arrived home safe feeling very thankfull to
our Heavenly Father for his mercies over us and famielies
while traveling over Two Thousand miles, also very thankful
to again enjoy the Society of our Famielies and freinds and
find them in good health

It was a long and grueling trip that included almost
every kind of nightmare. It consumed nearly five months of
Henry's life and represented a very large personal sacrifice.
He, like the others, had not only volunteered his time, but his
livestock and equipment as well.

Henry was home at last, and not a minute too soon.

(Sept.) 20   My wife Margaret brought me a fine son at sun
down, named him Henry William.

THE MID-1860S

Chapter Ten

It is unlikely that Henry rested, even after such a long trip. It was his nature to do the things that needed to be done.

His journal is sparse for the next few weeks, but we do know it snowed for the first time that fall on October 28. We also know he sat in on a bishop's court for an absent high councilman, and he received this word from abroad:

Dec 3, (1864) ...I got a letter from my Brothers in England[.] my Bro George had died on the 22 of Aug not in the church

This must have been sad news for Henry. Even though he had been expelled from George's home, he must have still loved him. He would have wished for his baptism. Henry could only hope George would accept the gospel somewhere beyond the veil.

There was an outbreak of measles in Logan. Both children caught them. Henry blessed Henry William on January 5, 1865. The only other January entry concerns the proposed tabernacle.

(Jan.) 9 I was sliding logs for our new Tabernacle which was in contemplation to be built 60 ft whide and 106 ft Long[.] to be built of Rock

Regardless of the weather, food for hungry mouths was still necessary. Obtaining it was a challenge.

Feby 10 (1865) I started to Brigham City to get me a grist ground[.] all the mills was froze up and had been for some time,[1] we had very cold weather this winter[.] I had to stop till the 12th for my grist, the snow was 6 ft deep going through the mountains[.] I caught a bad cold

It snowed for an entire week and covered the whole valley "to a depth of knee deep."

Henry continues:

(Feb.) 13 Henry Wm was taken very sick with convulsive fitts[.] I fasted and prayed and kept administering to him with the assistance of his grand fathers, on the 20th they left him and he was then alright and we felt very thankful that the Lord had heard and answered our prayers

Henry keeps us appraised of events concerning the Church as well as national events. He mentions that Brigham Young had purchased one of the Sandwich Islands to raise sugar, and a donation was taken up and money was sent to the States[2] to buy telegraph wire for a line from Logan to Saint George.

The next two journal entries he records are opposite extremes. For Henry, these events were probably of equal importance.

April 18, News came that Abraham Lincoln Prest of the U.S. had been assasinated in his Box in a theater and Sectry Seward and his son were wounded in their own house, this caused quite an excitement

April 24 I commenced plowing[.] we had a very late spring and a very hard winter before it all through the Teritory[,] and a great amount of stock died in some places

On one of their regular visits from Salt Lake City, brothers Wilford Woodruff and Franklin D. Richards

---

[1] There was no electricity, at that time, and the mills were run with water power.

[2] Utah was not a state yet, hence, the reference to "the States."

compared the favorable condition of the Saints now to when they were driven out of Nauvoo. George Albert Smith gave a history of the first settlements in the valleys. George Q. Cannon talked about home manufacturing and being prepared. President Young again exhorted the Saints:

> to stay at home and not be running to the mines.

Indians are mentioned less often and in more friendly terms. It is nonetheless apparent that some threat remained, for the militia were maintained in readiness; however, grasshoppers would soon replace Indians as the number-one problem.

Returning to Henry's journal, we find that on June 16:

> The mountains were covered with snow and snowed in the valley quite fast

> Aug 3 Prest Young and company came again to visit us and held a 2 days meeting

> (Aug.) 4 We had a grand review of the Military corps of the whole county and organized a Brigade[.] E. T. Benson General,...with other officers

> (Aug.) 5 Saturday, meeting commenced[.] the people coming in crowds from the other settlements, H. C. Kimball spoke of our Endownments and covenants that we had made, Said we could not mingle with the wicked and be justified before God, also cleanliness and Obediance[.] Prest Young spoke upon the necessity of having a telegraph line running through this valley, so that we may know the news at any time[.] said the wicked world was still opposed to this church and People[.] John Taylor exhorted the Saints to be faithful and live right before the Lord, and no nation would have power over this people for this Kingdom would not be given to another[.] at 5 P.M. a general inspection of arms was gone through with

> Aug 6 ...Prest Young advised the people to keep the spirt of Liquor out of their organizations for that would bring darkness, he invited all the choirs to attend the next fall conference in the City

(Nov.) 11 We went through a sham[1] Battle

(Nov.) 26 (1865) News came that [Name in original journal] had shot David Davidison near Franklin[.] he was brought home to Logan and lived until Dec 6 and then died

Dec 2, A City Police of 100 men was organized to guard the City and be on the look out

A court trial was held and David Davidison's killer was sentenced to ten years in the penitentiary.

A telegraph line became a priority. On December 7, a call came from Brigham Young asking for:

...cash to send back to the states to buy wire to put up a telegraph line to run through the teritory from the North to Dixie[2][.] this county to furnish $2000 and 7 teams

Another priority was to help the poor as they crossed the plains.

1866 Feby 4 We commenced to fit up our teams to go back for the poor[.] 500 was wanted for this season[.] 52 for this county besides the 7 for wire, our portion for Logan was 15[,] mostly mule teams from here...

The next several entries deal with sickness, bad weather, cold, and men who froze to death.

When time permitted, Henry worked on his adobe house. It was to be only 28 by 17 feet, but to him it was a castle.

On April 15, 1866, Henry makes reference to the wagon train heading east. He was not included this time.

Our teams rolled out in fine order

They still had to keep an eye on the Indians.

July 2, (1866) A circler was sent from Prest Young for us in the northern settlements to build forts in the small settlements

---

[1] Sham means fake.

[2] Dixie is the general area around St. George, Utah.

to guard our stock if the Indians should trouble [us] as they were doing in the south

July, August, and September were busy months, and the events varied considerably.

(Jul) 3 I was on guard riding around the country

(July) 8   I was blessd with another son[.] named him Thos McNeil Ballard[.] my wife got along well

(July) 10 Was hauling for 5 days to build a rock wall on the square for defence

(July) 14 A general training of all the valley at Logan

(July) 16 Commenced cutting my hay

(July) 18 I was on guard at the horse herd

27 Aug Went around the Ward for a donation for the Indians which was now freindly

Sep 2 Our teams got back again to Logan all well[1]

Sep 3 & 4 Helping to fitt up our Bowery and fence around it for a visit from Prest Young and party

President Young and company came for a two-day conference. He and several of the Brethren spoke on various gospel principles. More pertinent to the local Saints was Brigham Young's remark concerning the Indians:

...be kind to the Indians for the day was not far distant when they would be our freinds[,] but we must guard against them yet...

He also counseled the Saints:

...not to trade with the firm of Gilbert in S. L. City[,] but to encourage our berthern in trade

On October 14, 1866, Ezra T. Benson returned from the October conference to three inches of snow and gave a conference report to the Saints.

---

[1] He makes references here to the teams that left for Missouri the previous April to help the poor come west.

The later part of the month Henry spent four days doing military drills, two days setting up telegraph poles, and two days gathering cattle from the west side of Bear River. He then started for Salt Lake City to sell some wheat, but was driven back by rain and had to sell his wheat in Brigham City—and later:

Decr 1 I again started to S. L. City but it soon commenced raining again which made the road very heavy[1]

Dec. 8 It snowed and blowed all day[.] I got home again

(Dec.) 14 I went with some other Bretheren to explore the Logan Kanyon road that had been worked

(Dec.) 17 Commenced upon the Road in the Kanyon

Brother Benson, a member of the legislature, had just returned from Salt Lake City. He told the Saints:

the time had come for us to stop tradeing with our worst enemies.

In addition to the regular Sunday meetings, church was being held on Thursday evenings as well.

On January 28, 1867, Henry celebrated his birthday with a supper and dance in his new house.

On February 5, 1867:

A Business meeting was called and charter gotten up and company organized for Logan Kanyon Road[2]

Mar 17 A letter was read in the meeting on Sunday from Prest Young asking the Bishops to see that the people keep one years Breadstuff on hand as the country was full of Grasshoppers eggs laid last fall

---

[1] This is an interesting use of the word heavy. Henry uses it several times to describe road conditions.

[2] You may recall in an earlier entry that a company was to be formed to build a toll road in Logan canyon. For 50¢ one could use the road.

The subject of grasshoppers was brought up often enough for us to know they were a real menace. The insects had a sobering effect on Henry and his young family, as future entries will confirm.

We return to Henry's journal.

(Apr.) 25 (1867) I commenced to do a little in putting [in] my crops

July 24 We had a good time in celebrating the day[.] we got up a supper for all the poor that would come to it of Logan

Aug 4 A prayer Circle was organized with Bro E T Benson as Prest, it was held in an upper room in Bro Hezekiah Thatcher house[.] I was privelaged to be a member of the same

The grasshoppers had taken their toll on the crops, and money was tight for the Ballards.

(Aug.) 25 I started with [a] load of freight to Echo Kanyon to make a little [money] because the grasshoppers had eaten up the most of my wheat, in some places they had taken everything, it was only through the mercies of the Lord that we had raised any thing as the hoppers was so thick

The Brethren from Salt Lake were again in Cache Valley in early September. Henry, as usual, was helping to fix up the "bowery" for:

the reception of Prest Young and Party.

There were two days of meetings at the bowery, and the subjects taught ranged from testimony bearing to the children of Israel. The often mentioned "home manufacturing" is addressed again. The subject presented by Brigham Young was an interesting one.

(Sept.) 8 W Woodruff spoke upon the follies of many that left the church in an early day...[.] Prest Young spoke upon the order of the Priesthood and the causes of some leaving the church and of Oliver Cowdrey putting in the chapter upon Marriage in the Book of Doctrine & Covenants and not Joseph Smiths wish...

The Brethren from Salt Lake City soon left for meetings in the Bear Lake Valley. By September 15 there was snow on the mountains. That is a little early, even for Cache Valley.

Then on:

Octr 1   I started to S. L. City with my wife and her sister Emily McNeil and her Father to conference

We know from past entries that Henry generally had something planned in addition to conference when he traveled to Salt Lake City this time of the year.

This trip was no exception.

A TIME
OF TRIALS

Chapter Eleven

Fall conference was to be held on October 6, 1867. Henry and his party arrived in Salt Lake City on October 3, with plans for the next morning.

(Oct.) 4 Emiley McNeil received her Endowments and was sealed to me the same day

George Q. Cannon performed the marriage ceremony in the Salt Lake Endowment House. At Henry's insistance, Margaret witnessed the event.

Two days later they attended conference together on Temple Square.

(Oct.) 6 Conference commenced in the new Tabernacle[.] It was so large it was very hard to hear the speaker[.] the wind and dust blew very hard

(Oct.) 7 It rained the most of the day which made it very disagreeable but the house was mostly filled[.] Prest Young give the Bretheren texts to preach from, he wanted a donation taken up to bring the poor out from old England, he counciled the Young people to get married and about 150 Brethern to go to Dixy and settle[.] [Name in original journal] was cut off from the Quorum of the twelve for preaching false doctrine dening [denying] the power of the redemption. J F Smith son of Hyrum filled his place

89

(Oct) 9 Arrived home again safe

Once in Logan, Margaret shared her home with Emily, giving her a room to herself.

The Saints still felt a need for an active military. According to Henry, the militia engaged in a two-day military training session at the Church farm. It included another sham battle.

There were other real battles to be fought as well: accidents, untimely deaths, family tragedies, privations, and eventually an all-out war with the grasshoppers.

Nov. 5 Bro Joseph Waterson got hurt by a falling tree falling upon him in the Kanyon while cutting logs

(Nov.) 7 I set up with him all night

(Nov.) 10 He died at 3 p.m. after great suffering

(Nov,) 11   He was burried with great respect[,] 35 teams following his remains, also a company of Horse men[.] he was greatly respected by all[.] he was 23 years of age...

President Young was concerned about the poor and:

...requested the saints to pay in their fast day donations to support the poor and not draw so heavy upon the Tithing store

Jany 2, 1868 We met in the different Ward school houses on the fast day and the people donated to the poor.

(Jan.) 20 I was collecting means in my ward for 4 days for the P. E. Fund[1] to gather the poor from the old countries

The pioneers were not accident-prone people, but accidents did happen—some were very serious.

Feby 19 In coming down the Logan Kanyon my team and load slid off into the River falling over the bank about 29 feet

---

[1] P. E. Fund refers to the Perpetual Emigration Fund. It was a fund set up through private donations. The money was loaned to immigrants to come to America with the stipulation the money would be replaced so other immigrants could borrow from it. Thus, it became perpetual.

into 6 feet of water, but coming of[f] very lucky in not getting damaged much[.] I escaped alright

(Feb.) 25 I was helping to cut a ditch to turn more water into the north fork of the river from the south fork, and some Bretheren was at work repairing a brake in [the] upper ditch when the bank caved down killing Alexander McNeil and badly hurting James Beverland

(Feb.) 26 He was burried[.] I attended his funeral

By April 3, 1868, Henry was planting his crops. Brother Ezra T. Benson was again reporting to the Valley the messages of general conference.

President Young wanted the Saints to stop using pork and to keep the word of wisdom. Also, sixty teams from Cache Valley were needed to go back for the poor.

Helping the poor come west was now a lot easier for the teamsters. The terminus of the railroad had moved 500 miles west of the Missouri River, and continued to move westward. This was a real blessing for the drivers and animals—it saved 1,000 miles of travel.

A different kind of blessing was in store for Henry. Margaret, it seems, had endured a busy nine months. On May 15, 1868, Henry noted:

I was blessed by my wife Margaret bearing me a pair of twins[,] a Boy and Girl, Charles James and Jennett McNeil Ballard

A month later:

(June) 22 Prest Heber Chase Kimball, Died in Salt Lake City[,] aged 67 years

(June) 24 At 2 p.m. meetings were held althrough the teritory where the news could reach at the same time as the funeral services were being held in Salt Lake City where 8,000 people atttended

July 5 My twins were blessed[.] Charles James by his Gd father Thos McNeil[.] and Jennett McNeil by her Gd father Wm Ballard

91

(July) 6   A special fast meeting was called for the Lord to turn away the Grasshoppers from our crops...

Pioneer Days, on July 24, were always a cause for celebration. The people in the Valley enjoyed lots of good food, as well as the marching and fife[1] bands.

The Church authorities were on the way to Cache Valley, and, for the first time in years, Henry makes no mention of "working on the Bowery." He usually helped prepare it for their return. When they did arrive they met with local leaders, and organized a "School of the Prophets."

During one of the meetings, George Albert Smith advised the brethren to be sure and obtain their naturalization papers so they could vote and receive the benefits of the land laws. President Young, at the same time, counseled

...the young people to get married that was old enough and keep the laws of God[.] also for the saints to continue to donate to the gathering of the poor from the old countries[.] said if some did apostatize it was alright[.] he blest the saints in the Name of the Lord [and would] the people stop trading with their enemies[.] said he would make it a test of fellowship if they continued...

By mid-November, little Jennett was sick with the "Hoop-in-cough." In turn, all her brothers and sisters came down with it.

As money was scarce, hauling grain to sell in Box Elder County helped fill the near empty family coffers. The harsh winds and biting cold made it miserable for Henry during the three trips he made that November in 1868.

On January 2, 1869, Henry was headed west to the Logan river bottoms in search of livestock, and

...my horse broke through some Ice which was covered with 3 or 4 inches of snow[.] My horse fell down upon my right leg breaking it just above the ankle joint[.] I was 3 miles from

---

[1] An instrument similar to a flute, but higher in range.

home and alone, the small bone was not broken and by
seeking the Lord he give me strength to walk nearly home
before I got any help, but first I neary fainted and then
chilled[.] my horse got away and went home letting my
familey know that some thing was the matter[.] Bro David
Lamroux set the bone and the Bretheren administered to me
and I got along very well

(Jan.) 13 I set up in a chair for 3 hours and felt very thankfull
for that privilage

Feb 2 I was so far recovered that I was able to go out doors
to the stack yard by the aid of a crutch but not able to bear
much weight upon my foot

Still in a little pain, but managing, Henry attended the
School of the Prophets on March 20. Later that month he
was introduced to what could have led to a whole new
enterprise.

(Mar.) 27 Bro George D Watt of Salt Lake City preached to
us upon the subject of silk culture in Utah[.] he showed us
some raised in Utah[.] he had some Mulbery cuttings for
sale[.] I bought 100, but I never raised any trees

In early May the fall grain was just turning green, and
the grasshoppers were hungry.

May 4 The Grasshoppers commenced eating up my Wheat[.]
they where very thick thourghout the valley doing much
damage to the crops, in fact nearly taking every thing.

While not in attendance, Henry was well aware of an
event of national importance, an event that changed the face
of America forever.

May 10 The 2 great Railroads[,] the Union Pacific and
Central Pacific reaching from the Missori River to Calafornia
connected west of Ogden City[,] but afterward was so devided
to have the junction of the road at Ogden, a great celebration
was held at the spot where it was finished[1]

---

[1] This was the completion of the transcontinental railroad
connecting the nation, by rail, from coast to coast. The last spike
driven was made of gold. A celebration is still held each year in
commemoration of that great event.

The railroad was of great importance to the Church, and the leaders lost no time in getting it to Salt Lake City.

> (May) 17 Prest Young and his councilors broke the ground for the commencement of the Utah Central Railroad from Ogden to Salt Lake City 40 miles.

We don't know whether or not this was a new experience for Henry, but he spent several days shearing sheep at a cooperative sheep herd in Box Elder County. Upon returning home he

> found that the Grasshopers had eaten up nearly every green thing

Much of Henry's summer was spent attending meetings with the church officials from Salt Lake as they made a loop through Cache Valley, Bear Lake, and through the mountains to Franklin, Idaho. Bits of wisdom were disseminated, and again the subject of telegraph lines was brought up. President Young wanted the line extended through the mountains to Bear Lake. He also wanted the road through the canyon extended to Bear Lake.

While traveling to Ogden on business, Henry took time to see the trains. During the next few days he worked on the Logan Canyon road, cut what little was left of his hay, and celebrated the 24th of July.

One month later he was in Box Elder County again, trying to earn some much-needed extra cash.

> Aug 31 I went to Willard City to work upon a Thrashing machine that I had a share in[,] to work for my bread stuff[,] for the Grasshoppers had eaten up my wheat as they had done in other places[.] Also laying their Eggs for another years increase

> Sep 4 While at Willard I heard the news that Apostle E T Benson had Died very suddenly the evening before at Ogden City...

> 1869 Sep 5 He was burried with great respect

Henry had endured his share of trials during the last year, but there were more in store for him.

(Sept.) 10   I was telegraphed for to come home for my little girl Jennett was very sick

(Sept.) 11   I got home and found her very sick cutting her teeth and canker very bad, we done every thing for her that we could but still grew worse

(Sept.) 18   We was very much pained in having to give her up, she died at 9:30 p.m.

(Sept.) 19   She was burried in the Logan Cemetery at 4 p.m.

(Sept.)   24 (1869) My other little twin son Charles James was taken worse[.] he had been sick but had been getting better[.] he had the same complaint

(Sept.) 28   He Died at 7:30 p.m. 10 days lacking 2 Hours from the time of his Darling twin sister, they were two bright loving little children

(Sept.) 29   He was burried at 4 p.m. by the side of his sister

Octr 4   I was thrown out of my wagon upon the hard street falling upon the back of my head. I was stunned, but knowing that all of my children was in the Wagon I exhurted myself and caught hold of the lines of the horses and stoped them from running away when I then had to again drop to the ground, but through the kind hand of Providence I was not hurt much

In spite of the accident the day before, Henry was on his way to Willard to pick up the little bit of wheat he had worked so hard to harvest. It hadn't been properly stored, and he was concerned about it.

(Oct) 6   Returned home with my bread stuff and was very thankfull for it

By the end of October, 270 men were again working on the Logan canyon road. It had been pushed as far as Ricks Springs, so fine progress had been made.

Good progress was also made on the Logan Hall. By January 1, 1870, it was ready for use.

A month later Henry noted that President Young had wired that:

Trumbull was getting up a bill in congress to divide up the Utah Territory and attach it to Idaho Territory[.] we got up a pertition remonstrating against its passage

While trials were plentiful, there were also good days. February 12, 1870, was good day for Henry.

My Wife Emiley bear me a little Daughter[.] Named her Emiley Elizabeth, she got along well

More bills came before the legislature, bills that called for action on the part of the Saints.

April 5, We held a mass meeting in the Hall to protest against the bill gotten up before Congress by Cullum to punish all those that had entered into Poligamous marriages there by breaking up this people

April 9, 1870, was another one of those good days for Henry.

My Wife Margaret bear me a son, called him George Albert

The war with the grasshoppers was well under way, and the Saints devised a strategy to protect themselves against the insects.

(Apr.) 11 1870 I was helping to lay off a Ditch to enclose a cooperative wheat feild...we had all our wheat in 2 feild[s] so we could protect them from the Grasshoppers

Everyone was involved in the grasshopper war, including Margaret. An excerpt from her autobiography reads:

We also had grasshopper wars. I have seen the heavens darkened with grasshoppers until one would think it was midnight. I have gone out at such times and driven them into a trench with a bunch of willows and buried them alive. [Even] With all that we killed the ground would be left perfectly bare. They destroyed our crops and my husband had to go over into another valley and work on a threshing machine to get bread for the winter

On May 5, George Albert and Emily Elizabeth were blessed at fast meeting. About a week later Emily was ill. Presumably it was just a cold. Henry also had a cold and in mid-June he was ill with a sore throat—something he suffered from all too often.

On June 21, President Young and his party came to Logan—this time from Bear Lake. There were the usual two days of meetings.

One of the speakers, John Taylor, delivered a sermon on the trials of former-day Saints and said it was necessary to be tried. Brother Franklin D. Richards admonished the Saints to make improvements to their properties and to obtain machinery to make things easier and to save time. Apostle Brigham Young Jr. followed up by reminding them to fix up their fences and to get out from under dirt roofs. Brigham Young advised the Saints to keep the Word of Wisdom, as it was for their own good. Build factories, he told them, and take good care of your wheat. He went on to say that had the people been faithful, they would not have had to suffer with grasshoppers destroying crops. Finally, he admonished, if the Saints did not listen to the counsel of the servants of the Lord, the Lord would send other trials to "this people."

Henry knew a lot about trials. They had become a way of life for him. Would there be more?

July 30 My little daughter Emiley Elizabeth died

(July) 31 She was burried by the side of her little Brother and sister

Emily McNeil Ballard,
second wife of Henry Ballard

RAILROADS
TO THE VALLEY

Chapter Twelve

A telegram from Brigham Young began the 1871 year for the Saints. He wanted the bishops to stop taking tithing or doing any more tithing settlements until further notice.

In spite of the hardship a tax levy would impose on them, the people of Logan voted on April 1 to build and operate a school for the children. Henry and Margaret's children were definitely school age.

(Apr.) 6   I Baptized and confirmed my little Daughter Margaret Hannah

The ever-enterprising Saints met in the new Logan Hall to organize a cow pasture company. A president, other officers, and a secretary were chosen to solicit shares.

Peter Maughan, an early pioneer and the founder of Maughan's Fort (now Wellsville), had taken ill. A prayer circle was called in his behalf. Brother Maughan died a few days later on April 26, and then:

A very large concourse[1] of people assembled to pay their last respect to his remains...

---

[1] A crowd; throng.

Tithing was not always paid in cash. In the 1800s the Saints had little money. They usually paid with produce of some kind, such as hay, grain, or animals.

May 14 I started to Ogden with a load of Tithing

By July 2 Henry was ill with another sore throat, nevertheless, he spent the day

...gathering up lumber in the ward...to build a fence around the Hall...

(July) 17 Prest Young and company came into Logan from Bear Lake valley down through Logan Kanyon[.] they visited the settlements around till Saturday

(July) 22 Sunday, meetings commenced under the Bowery

(July) 23 Our meeting closed with good instructions from Prest Young

While the new Logan Hall was ready for use, they chose the bowery because it was cooler. It may have been too hot for note taking, for this is the first time Henry does not tell us the messages of the visiting General Authorities. The message could very well have pertained to railroads, for one month later:

Aug 23 A company was organized to build a railroad from Ogden to Soda Springs and shares were taken to commence work

(Aug.) 26 Ground was broken at Brigham City to connect there with the Central Pacific road for the present

(Oct.) 22 Sunday F D Richards preached to us in Logan Hall urging the Railroad building...Also telling us of the doings of Judges in Salt Lake City of the aresting of Prest Young[,] D H Wells and Geo Q Cannon and several others in Salt Lake City for Poligamy and other false charges, the 3 Brethern were bailed out under bonds to appear at appointed times, Prest Young telegraphed to F D Richards to be in Salt Lake City in the morning. I took him to Wellsville with my team after the nights meeting, I got back home at 1 in the morning

Octr 24 I started out to work upon the railroad

(Oct.) 25 My horses left me and went home

(Oct.) 26   I started back again and commenced work at Packs Springs

(Oct.) 28   It stormed so bad we had to come home

(Oct.) 30   I again started and took out my wife Emiley to cook for our company that we had working together[.] Robt Davidson and myself took a small contract on the other side of the mountain in Box Elder County[.] it was a very hard peice of work and hard to get men to go and work at it long at a time as it was only working for stock in the road[,] hence that was the reason that I took my wife out to cook and make it more comfortable for the men to continue to work

Nov 11   I went home to get more Provisions and feed[,] also to see my familey

1871 Nov 12   I went back again to the camp

(Nov.) 25   I again went home for more supplys, also some other teams with me and it snowed hard during the night[,] also the next day[,] Sunday[,] till it was 2 feet deep

(Nov.) 27   Monday it cleared off, and I started back with a sleigh to brake the road to get my wife and the men home but I could not proceed with it and had to turn back[.] and some of the men that had come home went on, on horse back untill they met them up in the mountains[,] trying to get through[.] They helped them along by braking the road for them as best they could, they all got home safe after dark, but very cold and tired, and I was very thankfull for I could not go on with the men on horse back because it always hurt me in doing so since I had my leg broken

Winter snow and bitter cold made it impossible for the Saints to do any more on the railroad that fall and winter. There were plenty of other things that demanded their attention.

Decr 10   Bishops Sheets of Salt lake City preached to us upon the paying of our Tithing, and to donate to the expences of the court upon the trial of Prest Young and his Brethern which was to come off in Jany 9, following

(Dec.) 11   I was visiting through the ward for Donations for that purpose

(Mar 4 ...our city Election came off and the Apostates got up an opposite Ticket but they did not accomplish any good

April 15 A telegram came from Washington D.C. stating that the doings of Judge J B. McKean in arresting Prest Young and the others, had been decided by the supream court of the United States to be illegal and unlawfull and ordered their release but the officers here paid no attention

President Young and the other Brethren must have been arrested for a second time. Henry's note, dated the previous October 22, 1871, stated they "were bailed out under bond."

April 25 Prest Young and the other Bretheren was released from custady on writ of Heabus corpus

May 1 They took an excurtion trip to Brigham City to see the new Railroad which had commenced to run a few miles

1872 May 17 I went down to Salt Lake City with some other Bretheren to prove up on our Government land

Octr 3 I Baptized my Son Henry William and Christian J Larsen Confirmed him, a council of the Bishops was called of Logan, to examian the Tithing Books and we found that a great many came short in paying up thier Tithing as they should

(Oct.) 6 At conference in Salt Lake City Prest Young spoke upon starting a city somewhere in the Territory after the Order of Enock...

Nov 14 It was a very cold bitter day[.] the Winter seemed fairly set in

Henry had made no mention of working on the railroad since November of 1871. He did, however, have a contract to do part of the work, and had been very involved the previous year. It is highly probable he was there working much of the time, and was about to go again, despite the aforementioned cold.

(Nov,) 25 I again went out onto the railroad to work, it was now in the valley[.] I was called home at night as my wife was sick

1872 Nov 26 My wife Emiley bore me a son which we called Willard Russell Ballard...

Dec 2 (1872) I again went out onto the railroad

(Dec.) 9 I again went back to the road on Monday and staid all week camping in tents

(Dec.) 16 Went back to work but came home nights as we was now getting nearer home

(Dec.) 20 My Wife Margaret was taken sick with a cold and sore throat. The Railroad cars got into Mendon[,] the first settlement in the valley[,] 8 miles from Logan

Dec 26 Margarets Quinsay[1] in her throat broke and she felt much better afterward

(Jan.) 31 The Engine and cars got into Logan in the evening

Feby 1 They give the school children a ride for a short Distance and back again

1873 Feby 3 A celebration of 3 parties for the arrival of the Railroad into Logan was given in the evening

As hard as the Saints had worked to get the railroad into Cache Valley, they certainly deserved a celebration of "3 parties."

---

[1] Quinsy is a serious inflammation in the throat, often leading to an abscess. Every joint in the body seems to ache. It is rarely contracted any more.

Left to right: Margaret, Henry, Emily

ROOTS OF
UNITED ORDER

Chapter Thirteen

The celebrations for the completion of the railroad were now behind the Saints—and the trains provided a valuable service for them. The telegraph lines were in and working well. In the near future, Brigham Young would launch a campaign asking the Saints to look at a new order.

Returning to Henry's journal:

(Feb.) 4   A large number of home missionaries was called to visit the different settlements and preach to the people on Sundays[.] I was called to be one of them

(Feb.) 6   Willard Russell was blessed at fast meeting by Christian J Larsen

(Feb.) 9   My wife Margaret bore me another son which we named Melvin Joseph Ballard

(Feb.) 14   [Name in origional journal] shot and killed David Crockett Junr without Provecation

(Feb.) 18   News started that the murderer [Name in original journal] was around in the City and we was soon on his tracts[,] for he had hid up since the shooting[.] he was followed down onto the River West for about 3 miles when he was surrounded and taken to the court house in Logan by the City Marshal, and the people was so enraged by the foul course that he had taken, as it was known that he had killed 3

105

persons before this one, some men rushed into the court house and brought him out and Hung him up to the sighn post in front till he was dead[1]

1873 Feby 19 David Crockett after suffering for a while Died and was burried on this day

Normally most of the snow in Cache Valley is gone by March; however:

March 10, The Bretheren turned out enmass and shoveled snow to open the Railroad track through the great snow drifts which had been blockaded for a week

(Mar.) 11 (1873) We got it opened through to Brigham City from Logan.

Three weeks later Henry blessed his son Melvin Joseph. He started planting his crops during that same time period, and on April 13 he went to Mendon to "preach."

From May 25 until the end of the month, Henry devoted all of his time to Church work. This included taking part of his family to Salt Lake City to do baptisms. The train was running, but Henry chose to travel by buggy. Perhaps the cost of so many train tickets was prohibitive.

May 25 I started to Salt Lake City taking my Wife Margaret and Daughter Margaret H[.] Also my Father and Mother and my Father in law and Mother in law and their son Thomas[.] Taking their team we all were going down to get baptized for our Dead relatives, we went to Willard City and staid over night with Bro McCartheys

(May) 26 Went to Farmington and staid at John Moons

(May) 27 Reached the City and staid at Wm Duncans

(May) 28 We got our Baptizing done for our Dead

---

[1] A full account of this incident was researched by Lucille Randall and published in the *Salt Lake Tribune* on Sunday, September 7, 1975. The main source of information was a detailed entry in the diary of Nick Crookston, the author's grandfather. He had been an eyewitness along with Henry.

(May) 29 We got the Sealing done and returned back as far as Farmington

1873 May 31 We arrived home again safe, and felt very thankfull that we had been able to do that work

After so many years in a buggy, the train must have been a blessing for the General Authorities. In late June they arrived by rail for another two days of meetings.

President Young was a busy man, and he wanted the Saints to be busy as well.

On June 28, 1873:

Prest Young said he wanted the saints to build their Tabernacle in Logan, and finish the Railroad to Franklin, and he wanted a Temple built in Logan, there was a Preisthood meeting held in the evening to talk over some matters

(June) 29 Sunday Prest Young spoke upon the office of a Patriarch[.] he said they would Ordain some in every large settlement, they Ordained five in Logan my Father was Ordained one...[he also] spoke upon the follies of the saints following the fashions of the Gentiles, and said he wanted the saints to prepare themselves for the order of Enock and blest the people

Henry spent very little time on recreation, but Independence Day was considered a good reason to celebrate, even though Utah was not yet a state.

1873 July 4 I took my familey up Logan Kanyon to spend the fourth with Prest Brigham Young Jr and the rest of the Logan Bishops, together with a large number of Bretheren and Sisters

Aug 5 Was cutting Hay on the church farm for 3 days for the church on tithing

(Aug) 8 Commenced harvesting my Barley

(Aug.) 11 Sunday went to Wellsville on Preaching mission

The General Authorities came to Logan for three more days of meetings. Again they arrived by train. It is abundantly clear the First Presidency wanted a temple in Logan.

(Aug.) 24   Joseph F. Smith spoke upon the necessity of the Temple being built in order that the work for Dead may be accepted of the Lord[.] said the people were abundantly able to build it...

The General Authorities then made the usual loop, by buggy, this time going up Blacksmiths Fork Canyon and back to Logan by way of Soda Springs.

Henry's journal is silent from September 6 until February 6, 1874. On that date he was invited to travel with Bishop Preston and others to Ogden to celebrate the completion of the Utah Northern Railroad from Brigham City to Ogden.

The railroad continued to grow, and by February 9, 1874:

Track laying was commenced at smithfeild to push it onto Franklin by March[.] We were busy hauling rock for the Tabernacle

Mar 2   Bishop William Hyde of Hyde Park Died[.] the Election of our city officers came off[.] the Apostates were again busy[.] They[1] only got 106 votes to 421 of ours[.] Governor Wood, appointed John Nelsen[,] an Apostate[,] for Probate Judge in Place of Wm Hyde, we got up a pertition to the Governor to appoint Bishop M D Hammond of Providence for Probate Judge

Mar 11   I got my leg hurt hauling rock for the Tabernacle by getting it caught between the sleigh and a rock after I had got my load off on the Square

(Mar.) 16   The Bretheren started out to shovel snow to get the Railroad track opened which had been blockaded for a month, we had so much snow this winter and drifted so bad, they could not keep it opened, they had opened it several times[.] we had a very hard winter[.] we had to drive the Tithing cattle out of the valley to keep them alive for the Hay

---

[1] The apostates.

was so scarce in the valley, and a great many sheep had already died with the cold without sheding or little feed[1]

(Mar.) 21 I went to get my sheep home from where I had them out on shares for they were dieing so fast[.] the snow was 2 feet deep on the level, I had to haul them home in sleighs[.] They got so weak one third of them had already died

Margaret was with Henry on that fateful day and remembers it this way:

...we had about one hundred sheep wintering in Clarkston. Since it was a very hard winter and the snow was very deep nearly all of them were dying. A man came and told my husband that if he wanted to save any of the sheep he would have to go at once with a wagon and haul them into shelter.

I told my husband to get another wagon and team and I would drive with him. He did not want me to go but I insisted for I felt so sorry to lose so many sheep and thought we could have double the number with the two wagons. I also thought I could be company for him on such a long drive. It was very cold. We started very early and it was eleven o'clock when we got home that night. We brought twenty sheep back with us but about half of them died on the way home. I never will forget the sight of so many sheep lying around dead and dying. It made my heart ache to see the suffering of these animals.

Referring back to his March 16 entry, Henry notes:

1874 Mar 23 The Bretheren got the Railroad opened

In April Henry helped lay track between Smithfield and Richmond and also got some plowing done.

The Brethren in Salt Lake City asked the Saints in Cache Valley to join the United Order[2] of Enoch. It was

---

1 Henry means there was no shed to put the sheep in.

2 United Order, "As then attempted, practice of the full law of consecration called for the saints to consecrate, transfer, and convey to the Lord's agent all of their property with a covenant and a deed which cannot be broken." (D. & C. 42:30; 58:35.) "They were given stewardships to use for their own maintenance, with all

similar to the Order some had entered into in Southern Utah. Apostle Erastus Snow came from Salt Lake City to help organize it, and a president and other officers were elected. When President Young spoke about it, he

> [Pointed] out to us very clearly the utility of the United order and said the Lord required obedience of his saints to that order

A committee was appointed to appraise the land for its value, presumably for the United Order. While the order is mentioned frequently for the next few years, it required a little promotion by the General Authorities before it was readily accepted.

Returning to Henry's journal we find that on:

> (June) 13 My brother in law Joseph McNeil Died of scarlet fever, which was very bad in some families[.] my children came down with it very bad

> July 7 My Son Geroge Albert died with it after being sick with it for some time and had commenced to get better but soon took a turn

> July 8 1874 He was burried[.] the weather was very hot and a large commet was to be seen every night for some weeks, and some of my children was very sick[,] especially my Daughter Margaret H[.] my little Boys body was taken into the room for my Girl to see him for the last time, all the faith of us as a familey and many of the Bretheren that came in was exercised for our childen but it seemed that these 2 loving children was not to be parted for very long from each other

> (July) 13 My Daughter Margaret Hannah Departed to join her little Brother, it was sad to have to part with them, but they are now gone to their rest in their purity, the other children was now some better

> (July) 14 She was burried beside her Brother

surpluses reverting back to the Lord's storehouses." Bruce R. McConkie, *Mormon Doctrine* (Salt Lake City: Bookcraft, 1966), p. 158

President Young visited Logan to leave instructions and talk of the United Order. Henry baptized his eight-year-old son Thomas. Thomas E. Ricks was indicted for polygamy and sent to prison to await trial.

Henry's family was growing. Another son was a gift from Emily on November 28, 1874. They named him Franklin Hyrum. He was blessed by his Grandfather Ballard the next day.

Apostle John Taylor traveled to Logan on January 2, 1875, and spoke again on the United Order by

...saying we must come to it in a small way at first

On February 16, 1875, there was another disaster.

Bro Wm K Robinson met with a fatal accident in Logan Canyon by being struct with a log while sliding timber, he was brought home and died in about half an hour afterwards, he was a good man and much respected by every one. Bro George Benson was also much hurt by the same log but he got better....

Thomas E. Ricks was a highly respected man in the valley. Now out of prison, he was being indicted for killing a horse thief fifteen years earlier. The deceased, David Skeens, when caught, had been held in the log schoolhouse. Henry had spent a night guarding him.[1] On another night, while Thomas E. Ricks was guarding him, he attempted a getaway by overpowering Ricks. Ricks shot him in self defense.

A trial date was set and a number of brethren, including William Ballard, Henry's father, traveled to Salt Lake City as witnesses on behalf of Ricks. Judge McKean, who had shown little sympathy for Mormons, was presiding. He put the trial off for an additional three weeks, then proceeded to arrest Brigham Young, and

---

[1] It was the night of June 29, 1860. See Henry's entry on page 45.

...fined [him] $25.00 and 24 hours in prison for not complying with Judge McKeans wims and notions

In the meantime both a new judge and a new governor had been appointed. They seemed much more friendly than the previous two. The trial was continued and on March 23:

We got a Dispatch in the evening stating that T E Ricks was acquitted although his enemies tried hard to have him convicted.

Then on

(Mar.) 25 The Brass band and great numbers of Bretheren and sisters turned out at the Depot to welcome Bro Ricks home again[.] he felt well in body and spirits and we all felt well to greet him

Turning back to March 17, 1875, Henry notes another tragedy.

A very large snow slide came down the mountain in Dry Canyon south side of Logan river, and caught Bro Israel J Clark and 2 of his boys in it, but him and one of his boys got out alright but the other one Israel J Junr could not be found, we got word of it in Logan and about 100 men turned out with shovels and after diging about half an hour we found him under about 2 ft of snow with his face down ward quite dead, a great many had shared the same fate this winter in Different parts of the Territory

It was again time for spring conference in Salt Lake City. With tracks installed and a train depot in Logan, it was much more convenient for Henry to attend. The General Authorities' messages are both interesting and pertinent.

(Apr.) 6 Conference commenced in the new Tabernacle[.] D H Wells was the first speaker[.] he spoke comparing the work of the Anciant saints with this latter day work, advised us to be self supporting as a people[.]...Orson Hyde gave good advice to the children which was assembled to sing some selected peices before the conference[.] he advised the parents to look well to their children[,] to keep them from breaking the sabbath[.] Geo Q Cannon spoke upon the same subject and was not in favor of free schools[,] showing its bad effects

1875 April 7 Prest Young said he was not in favor of free schools, he showed very plainly the need of the children learning the laws of life and how to make a living as well as book learning[.] he said he wanted our Legeslature next winter to spend their time for the people and board themselves and let the Government give their money to the Dogs and Wolves whom they thought the most of, he said this people knew the way to walk and go right ahead, Erastus Snow spoke upon the bad policy of people going into debt withought having the means to pay[.] said it would bring ruin to any people

(Apr.) 9 ...a large number of missionaries were called, the weather had been very cold and stormy nearly the whole conference an it was still continued for 2 days more, but I started home on the 10th

Henry started putting in his crops after conference. Two weeks later one of his horses was gored by a bull, which left him short an animal—it was one of a team.

While it seemed spring had arrived early, it still snowed on May 7.

On June 5, Brigham Young and his party arrived for two days of meetings. Henry makes no further comment about those meetings, but:

Brigham Young Junr spoke in our Preisthood meeting and told us that Prest Young had called upon the saints in Sanpete County to renew their covenents by Baptism by compling with the rules of the united order, and all of the Quorum of the Twelve that was there[,] 7 in all[,] went forth and was Baptized by D H Wells and confirmed by Prest Young, and a vote was taken in the meeting here to see who was willing to comply

Henry was ready to comply—he was baptized and confirmed that same day.

On the following day

there was a great number of the Brethern and sisters Baptized

By July 11, Emily and her son, Thomas, along with Henry William were baptized. The United Order was beginning in Cache Valley.

113

While not connected with the Order, Henry commenced cutting tithing hay on the church farm in late July. They put up nearly forty tons.

In mid-August President Young was in Logan. He told the Saints to finish the tabernacle and to be prepared to build a temple. He also:

> ...counciled us to faithfullness in all our duties for the Devil could get us to doubt in any duty or council[.] he would finally overcome that person if possable, as he had many before

Hauling sand for the tabernacle consumed August 17 for Henry. The next day he commenced harvesting his grain.

George Albert Smith died on September 1, 1875. Henry was unable to attend his funeral as it was held in Salt Lake City.

Another visit from the Brethren came on September 12. The main theme centered on parents watching after their children. Of course, the United Order was again mentioned.

The militia was still active:

> (Sept.) 16 Our 3 Days Drill commenced

And then:

> (Sept.) 19 My Wife Margaret bore me another Daughter[.] we named her Ellen Pheabe

> (Nov.) 3 The Teachers visiting Quorom was organized in the second ward of Logan City of Bretheren that had been Baptized into the United Orderd

The Second Ward was Henry's ward, and based on his journal, it was required that one be rebaptized into the United Order. Henry had been baptized on July 3, 1875, for that purpose.

The United Order was now established in Cache Valley. Henry was among the first to accept it.

> 1875 Dec 2, We held a meeting in our Ward to take into consideration the adviseability of sending to the States for a

turning lathe to make Broom handles as there was none in the Territory and to cooperate together as a ward and form a company to do all kinds of Wood work

(Dec.) 8 We held another meeting and Organized by forming a company of all those that took shares and agreed to send for the Broom handle factory and what other machnery was needed to carry on a Home Manufactury in Wood, also took into the company Bro C W Card and sons Saw Mill and lathe and shingle Mills. Bro P N Peterson and sons turned their Planeing Mill in as stock and we made arraingments to attach the Broom handle Lathe to the same Water Power, the Bertheren all felt well in Uniting together

1876 Jan 15   Bros Joseph F Smith and F. M. Lyman came from Salt Lake City and called a Bishops meeting to lay before us the views of Prest Young with regard to calling Missionaries to go and make settlements in Arizona Territory, 200 men was called from Utah and 25 was wanted from Cache County and 10 from Logan City[,] all to be ready to start by the last of the month, in the evening J F Smith give a lecture upon the History of Joseph Smith the Prophet, he said in 15 years the time would be up when the Lord told Joseph that he should see him, but it must be by him going to him in the sprit world

Jany 16 1876   They held another meeting urging us to be united in all things, the Bretheren of Logan was called[.] they all responded[1]

On January 17:

I was helping the Bretheren to get fitted up for the trip, we had a great deal of snow and cold

Later, on February 1:

They started out upon their journey

It was January 16, 1876, when these Saints were asked to leave their established homes and move again to an unknown place. Within two weeks they had disposed of

---

[1] The author assumes this refers to the men called to leave Cache Valley and settle in Arizona.

property, packed wagons and were on their way. What faith. What obedience to a prophet.

On February 3, Henry and several others traveled to Salt Lake City to get their naturalization papers. Henry was now a citizen of the United States of America. It had been 24 years since he had left England.

The winter had been a severe one. It had cost the lives of many cattle throughout the entire valley, but by the third week in April the Saints were able to plant crops.

On May 8:

> My wife Margaret was Baptized[1] by Joseph M Wight and confirmed by her Father[.] she was not able to be Baptized when the rest of the familey was

The problems with Indians were not yet over, but they had taken on an entirely different aspect.

> (May) 11 I went with some other Bretheren of the second Ward into Bear River and put in five acres of Wheat for the Indians, it was designed to put in 100 acres by the County

Mid-July brought Lorenzo Snow, Franklin D. Richards, and others to Cache Valley for another two-day conference. They talked more about the United Order, the building of temples, and doing work for the dead. July's end found the Saints again remembering and celebrating the day the Mormons came to Utah.

It was early August when Henry and other ward members put up 30 tons of tithing hay at the Church farm.

The grasshoppers, like the Indians, still remained a problem, but not of the same magnitude as in the past.

> (Aug.) 11 I commenced Harvesting my Wheat which was a very good crop, the grasshoppers made their appearance

---

[1] Margaret was baptized as a child. Henry is probably referring to the family's baptism into the United Order the previous July 11. See p. 113.

again upon us from the North, they had eaten up the crops in Marsh valley north

Octr 20 My wife Emily bore me another son[.] we named him Ernest Reid Ballard

Ernest was blessed a week later in Henry's home by his Grandfather McNeil.

The Saints' testimony of the United Order and their determination to have a temple are evident in the next few journal entries.

Dec 7 We held meetings in each Ward of Logan to take up a subscription to see what each one would donate towards the building of a Temple in Logan City[,] which this county together with Bear Lake, Malad, and Box Elder counties was called upon last conference to Build it, the people felt well toward it, there was also one to be built in San Pete County[.][1] raised $2119.00 for the first years payment

1877 Jany 22 to the 26 was very cold[.] it froze the north fork of Logan River solid turning it out of its channel onto the Island all around some houses[2]

(Jan) 27 The Basement story of the Logan new Tabernacle was Dedicated by F D Richards[.] it was a very cold day[.] we held a 2 Days meeting in it[.] Bros John Taylor, Lorenzo Snow, F D Richards, Charles W Penrose and Bisop L W Hardy preached to us upon the principles of the United Order[,] saving of our Grain, Building of Temples, Baptism for the Dead, and to respect the Houses Dedicated to the Lord, and the order of the Preisthood and of true Siecence [science] agreeing with the word of the Lord and his servants on earth

Jany 29 Our United Order Manufactering Company that we Organized one year before in the 2nd Ward had proved a

---

[1] This was to be the Manti Temple.

[2] In those days, Logan River forked near the mouth of the canyon and reconnected a few miles downstream. The portion of Logan on the inside became known as "the Island." While today this condition no longer exists in the same way, this area is still known as the Island.

success, and we had increased by attaching a Moulding machine to our other machinary and we now felt the need for a Branch Store connected with our Business

(Jan.) 30 The 3rd Ward joined with us and turned in their cooperative Dairy and took stock in our store[.] I was helping to lay off the ground to commence at once to build a store 18 by 24

(Jan.) 31 We commenced to dig the celler, but we had to first scrape the snow away and in about 25 Days we had it built and opened out to sell goods[.] it was a frame building

The St. George Temple had been under construction for some time. Late in February Brigham Young Jr. came to Logan from St. George where he had been with his father. Church authorities, he said, had dedicated a part of the temple on New Year's Day and were using it to give endowments. The rest of the building would be finished and dedicated in time to hold the April 6, 1877, conference in it.

In Cache Valley the vestry rooms of the nearly completed tabernacle were finished. Two more prayer circles were organized for a total of four in Logan. Henry was asked to preside over one of them.

The winter had been a little less severe in Cache Valley.

(1877) (Mar.) 23 I commenced to put my crop in, the winter having broken up sooner this spring, it had been the best Winter with the exception of 4 Days in Jany that we had ever had in this valley since it had been settled in 1859 or since the settlements had been made outside of what had been called Maughans Fort, which had been settled previouss to this date

May 5 I went to our United Order Dairy over on the West side of Bear River[1]

---

[1] Bear River flows down the west side of Cache Valley. It cuts through the mountains into Box Elder County a little north of Benson. The dairy he refers to was in Cache Valley. This is a reference to the actual Bear River, not to the city of Bear River.

The United Order is mentioned in Henry's writings only a few more times. He does not say how long it survived.

It was now time to move on to a new and even more exciting project.

THE
TEMPLE ERA

Chapter Fourteen

The Salt Lake Temple had been under construction for almost as long as the Saints had been in Utah. The St. George Temple was completed in early 1877. A temple in Logan had been talked of for years—then on

> (May) 16 Prest Young and a number of the Twelve Apostles came to Logan on the noon train

> (May) 18 The ground was Dedicated with Prayer by Orson Pratt for a Temple upon the hill over looking Logan City, Prest Young and John Taylor made some good remarks relating to the Temple and our duties to each other and our Dead friends[.] it was a very cold snowy day and had snowed in the night previous and it was now 4 inches deep, but the time had been set for 12 on that day, and it was attended to

Just a month after the completion of the St. George Temple, the construction of the Logan Temple was officially begun. It was May 18, 1877.

Since President Young and several of the Apostles were in Logan, it was a natural thing to hold a conference.

> (May) 19 Our Conference commenced[.] Bro F. D. Richards spoke upon the building of Temples and our duties to the Dead, in the afternoon Prest Young spoke upon many of the first doings of the church and its members, and how the

Gospel had made the hearts of many to rejoice, in the evening Erastus Snow give us a good Discourse upon the Order of the Preisthood

(May) 20 Orson Pratt dwelt largely upon the anciant records saying that when the Lord saw fit to reveal them there would be tons of them that we had never seen[,] and we would then understand more with regard to how the Nephites lived the United Order in their day....in the evening the Twelve Apostles called the Bishops together in the Logan Hall and ordained 12 of the Bretheren that had Been acting as such before but had not been ordained,[1] Apostle John Taylor ordained me a High Preist and set me apart as Bishop of the second Ward of Logan City, and we were to choose 2 councilors each so that we could hold a Bishops court when needed

Henry had been acting as bishop for years. It was April 20, 1861, when he was called to that position. Little did he realize it would be sixteen years and one month before he would be set apart and asked to choose his counselors.

Stakes were not part of the Church in Cache Valley yet, but:

May 21 Monday a meeting was called to organize this stake of Zion according to the pattern given to Joseph Smith[.]... Mosses Thatcher was appointed and set apart by Prest Young as Prest of this stake of Zion and Wm B Preston his first and with Milton D Hammond as his second councilors, and gave instructions to complete the organization of the stake....

Other things were discussed in that meeting, and President Young also gave the Saints a timetable for completion of the temple.

...He wanted us to go to work at the Logan Temple right away, he said he would give us 3 1/2 years to build it, but said we could build it in 2 1/2 years, he wanted it built as a free will offering to the Lord without mentioning wages[.] he Blessed the saints, and started back to Salt Lake City at 2 PM on the Train

---

[1] There were no stakes in Cache Valley at the time so there could have been twelve acting bishops, or perhaps Henry meant several bishops and their counselors were set apart.

Continuing, Henry notes on May 22:

I was signing a lot of United Order currency as I was President of the same, it was much more conveniant than orders, as we were doing a big business in the employment of a great many men and teams in loging and the Lumber Business.

Ten days after the dedication of the ground for the temple the first physical work was done.

May 28 Myself and other Bretheren commenced to plow and Scrape out for the foundation of the Logan Temple

On June 24, there was a killing frost in Cache Valley. President Young, accompanied by his son John W. Young, made his final trip to the Valley. On June 30, Henry ordained his son, Henry William, into the Aaronic Priesthood and set him apart as a deacon.

Henry returned to temple construction again on July 10. He helped open up a sand bank, and that night brought a load of sand to the temple grounds. It was the first load used on the temple.

The balance of July was spent harvesting Henry's hay and grain.

On August 29, Henry penned this entry.

Prest Brigham Young Died in Salt Lake City at his home after one weeks sickness at 4 P.M. it cast a gloom over the whole people

And then:

Sep 1 Saturday I went to Salt Lake City with a great many others to attend his funeral

(Sep) 2 Great crowds of people went to the New Tabernacle to see him where he had been taken the Day before the services commenced at 12 N. it was a great gathering, it was estimated that 30,000 people assembled on the occasion, [occasion] the saints felt to acknowledge the hand of the Lord in taking away their President although it was hard, every thing went off very orderly, the different grades of the Preisthood followed in their order in the great procession, I felt very thankfull that I had the privilage of being one in the number, he was highly esteemed by all of the saints and many of the outside world for he was kind to all that come into his company

On September 12, 1877, Apostles Wilford Woodruff and Brigham Young Jr. came to Logan for an evening meeting. The life of the Prophet Joseph and the labors of President Young were discussed. Brother Woodruff addressed the work for the dead and recounted how the Lord helped him to find names of his kindred dead.

Henry organized the deacons quorum and set apart his son Henry William as president on September 16. The next day:

> The corner stones of the Temple was laid, the Twelve Apostles laid the South East, Bishops and Lesser Preisthood laid the South West, High Preists and Presidents of the Stakes laid the North West, and the Prests [Presidents] of the Seventies laid the North East corners, a very large company assembled to witness the imposing ceremonies, 8 of the 12 apostles were present on the occation [occasion]

Late in 1877 the United Order was still intact.

> (Nov) 13 I was hauling a load of Doors for our United Order, and while unloading them in the rock building the cellar door was open and in steping backwards I fell down backwards 7 feet, hurting my leg but very fortinatly it did not hurt me worse

As Henry grew older, his journal entries were fewer in number. Many interesting things must have taken place, but Henry elects not to mention all of them. Some that he does mention center around family and Church matters.

His first entry for 1878 mentions "we had a good time" at the quarterly conference.

On January 28, some ward changes were made.

> We organized an acting Priests Quorum in our Ward, calling Will[ia]m Ballard my father and [other] bertheren to that position...

And on February 8, 1878:

My Wife Margaret bore another Daughter we called her Rebecca Ann Ballard

(Feby) 17, I Blessed her at the house

April 4, I again Blest her in the fast meeting

Exactly one month later it was time for quarterly conference again, and Henry penned his next entry.

May 4, Our Quarterly conference commenced[.] Bro E Snow said this valley was as a desirable place to live in as any place he had seen in these mountains[.] he said it was necessary for every man that presided over Quorum or Branch or Familey to be a revelator to such at all times, Bro Woodruff...refered to our dead[,] especially our young men that died occasionally[.] he said the Lord had need of them in the spirit world to carry on his work[.]...Prest J Taylor said he was well pleased with the reports of this stake

(1878) May 5, Bro F. D. Richards spoke upon the duties of the saints in attending to their prayers, Bro J F Smith bore a powerful testimony upon the principel of Celestial marriage[.] said it was obligatery upon the saints to fullfill that law for it was revealed from God for the exultation of the latter day saints, but it would damn those that practized it for a lustfull desire, but the Lord would bless those that obeyed it in reightousness[.] Prest J Taylor spoke at great length upon the order of the Preisthood[.] said that men must magnify it or give it up, was well pleased with the labors of the saints upon the Logan Temple and did not wish to oppress the people, but exhorted them to do all that they could and live in kindness in their families, and never do or say any thing before their children that they would be ashamed of, and blessed the people, Bro Woodruff encouraged the Elders to prepare themselve to preach the Gospel or do any other duty in the Kingdom of God

These messages were important to Henry. It appeared, from his past, that he took all of the precepts expounded by General Authorities to heart.

Quarterly conference convened again on August 3.

The upper story of the Logan Tabernacle was opened and our Qurately Conference was held therein, we had a good time[.] 9 of the apostles were present, they deposited the Church

125

Papers published in Utah, and some of the church works and other records in a stone box in the south East corner of the Logan Temple

Zion continued to grow.

Sep 9, My Wife Emiley bore me another Daughter, we named her Lydia Jane Ballard

Nov 7 I Blessed my Daughter Lydia J

Soon it was 1879, and spring must have been early.

Feby 26, I commenced to put my crop in

And on

April 10, I was taken very sick with severe pains in my Kidneys going to the Bladder[.] it lasted for about 5 hours

During general conference in Salt Lake City, Moses Thatcher, of Logan, was called to fill the vacancy occasioned by the death of Orson Hyde. Cache Valley now had two Apostles among the General Authorities.

A month after general conference, it was again time for quarterly stake conference in Logan. Bishop William Preston was sustained as stake president.

On May 5, 1879, Henry penned the following:

I went to Salt Lake City with some other Bretheren to escohrt Bro D. H. Wells from the Penitentuary where he had been confined for 3 Days because he refused to answer the Judges their questions put to him about the Endowment house[.] there was a large procession upon the occasion

Henry made no further journal entries until October 5, 1880. He had been to Salt Lake City and

...attended one of the best conferences that I ever attended, John Taylor as Prest of the Quorun of the Apostles was sustained as President of the church of Jesus Christ of Latter Day Saints...

The Church had been without a president for three years and one month.

Continuing on:

Nov 4 My wife Emily bore me another Daughter[,] we named her Jenny Lula

Early in December:

The Female releif society was reorganized in the second Ward[.] My wife Margaret was chosen by the sisters as Prest,...

Henry ended 1880 with another attack of kidney stones, or "gravel" as he called them.

Dec 31 I was again taken very sever with pains in my Kidneys also the gravel which lasted for 2 hours

The first Sunday of the new year, 1881, Henry blessed his little girl. Shortly thereafter a four-day ordeal occurred that only Henry himself can describe.

(Jany) 10, I started to Temple saw mill in Logan Canyon for a load of lumber with other bretheren for the Temple[,] a distance of 26 miles, after we started it commenced to snow and blowing the snow very bad[,] drifting the roads full, we had hard work to get through some of the drifts[,] but we got there about 4. P.M., it still snowed and blowed all night, blocking us intirely in

(Jany) 11 We shoveled snow and got our sleighs with a little lumber on them 2 miles down[,] and then took our teams back to the Mill for the Night[,] and about 10 P.M. 2 men came into camp from Logan[.] they had to leave their teams and come on foot wadeing the river in some places for 2 miles to miss the snow slides[.] they sent one man back to Logan to get men to come and help get us out of the snow

(Jany) 12 We started by packing our bedding upon our Horses and leaving our sleighs[.] we had to walk and brake the road for our Horses to travel, and it was still snowing and Blowing badly till noon when it commenced to rain, the snow was sliding which made it very dangerous[.] we had to be very carefull to avoid being caught, and in order to continue our travel we had to climb onto the sides of the mountains in places, we had to drive our Horses for 2 miles down the bed of the river in one place where the snow had slide so deep and too soft to bear them up, but we could walk upon it ourselves, in some places it slid into the river compleatly

127

daming it and turning it out of its bed for a while before the water cut its way through, afterwards leaving a bridge of snow[.] about 2 P.M. we met the Bretheren from Logan with supplies and to help us brake the road through, we were all very pleased to meet each other, as we were now out of the most dangerous part of the Canyon, we went on down to the Forks and made ourselves as comfortable as possable under a hanging rock[1] and at some shanties[2]

(Jany) 13 We all reached home safe, and found our families and freinds and the comunity at large had been very anxious watching and praying for our safe return, we all felt very thankful together that the Lord had so mericalously preserved us from the many dangers that we had been exposed to both seen and unseen, 2 Bretheren had been killed by a snow slide the winter previous on the same road

Henry's dedication and determination, and that of men like him, cannot be questioned.

Henry chronicled little for the rest of the year, but he did mention:

(Feby) 6 Prest J Taylor and J. F. Smith and W. Woodruff gave us some very pointed remarks upon the law of Tithing[,] also the word of wisdom, together with other good instructions

(Feby) 9 I Baptized and confirmed my 2 sons. Willard Russell and Melvin Joseph, they being 8 years old...[3]

Jun 10, I was kicked by one of my horses very bad in the right side while feeding[.] I was not able to work for a few days

---

[1] The "hanging rock" is twelve miles up Logan Canyon at Right Hand Fork. It is known today as Hanging Rock Cave. Henry's son, William Henry, loved to take his family there years later for family picnics and Dutch-oven cooking.

[2] Chinese workers were used in the production of railroad ties for the Utah & Northern Railroad. They built a row of shanties for living quarters about one-half mile above Hanging Rock Cave. It is now called China Row Picnic Area. It is probable these were the shanties Henry refers to.

[3] Willard Russell is the son of Emily. Margaret gave birth to Melvin Joseph.

Henry finished the year with this happy note:

Dec 13 My wife Margaret bore me another Daughter[.] we named her Lettie May Ballard, she was very sick with very hard labor[,] but she got along very well after her confinement

Almost three years pass without a single entry from Henry. He finally breaks the silence in May 1884.

(May) 14 Prest J Taylor and party came to Logan for the purpose of Dedicating the Temple

Even though Brigham Young "said he would give us 3 1/2 years to build it," it had taken one day less than seven years from the dedication of the ground to the dedication of the temple. During this same period the Saints of Cache Valley had some commitments to the Salt Lake Temple that had to be met. It is a wonder the temple was completed in so little time.

Like the other temples, the Logan Temple was made from local materials[1] and stands as a monument to the efforts and sacrifices of those hardy pioneers.

---

[1] Most of the rock was quarried in Green Canyon, six miles north and east of the temple. The discarded rock pile is much like it was years ago. The old rock foundations, laid for shanties, are gone. The quarry is referred to as the "Red Rock Quarry."

A sawmill was constructed about four miles up Temple Fork Canyon (of Logan Canyon) in September of 1877, to supply timber and lumber for the temple. It also supplied ties for the Utah & Northern Railroad.

Sawmill workers, about 30 in number, were paid in mill products and were thus able to build their own homes, granaries, and other buildings.

It is estimated that during the period of operation the mill produced more than two and one half million board feet of lumber, 21,000 railroad ties, 900,000 laths, two million shingles, 50,000 pickets, charcoal and an uncounted number of broom handles. (The broom handles were probably turned on Henry's broom handle lathes: see 1875 Dec 2 entry, page 114.)

A conference was held just prior to the ceremony, and it was well attended as Saints came from all over for the occasion.

> (May) 17 The Temple was dedicated at 10:30 A.M.[.] we had a glorious time[,] the different Preisthood being repersented in their order, Tickets of admission was issued to the various officers in the church for the first day and it was crowded to its utmost capacity

> May 18 The Bishops was given the privilage of inviting a certain number of the worthy saints from each Ward[.] and the Dedicatory prayor was again read, as it was written some what after the manner of the one given at Nauhvou Temple[.] it was again crowded and we had another good time, but Prest Taylor thought there was a lot more saints would like to have the privilage of witnessing the cerimonies

> (May) 19 The invitations was again extended to enough more worthy saints to again fill the house[,] and the same prayer was again read, and long services held as before on the two previous days, and it was a time long to be remembered by all that had the privilage of attending for truly the spirit and power of God was there, and the Bretheren told us that it had been made manifest to them that God had accepted of the House as built to His name[,] and it would be opened at once to give endowments to the living and the Dead[,] and they wanted the worthy saints to come on and do their own work[,] and also for those of their relatives that had died

> May 21, The Temple was opened for ordinances

Henry wasted no time in getting to the temple.

> June 4, I commenced to do Temple work for my Dead[.] my Wifes Margaret and Emily went also, My Father and Mother went a few times but they were too feeble to stand it long and they was counciled to turn the balance of the work over to me

---

The mill ceased operating in December of 1883 and burned to the ground in the winter of 1885–86. (Source: Sons of the Utah Pioneers plaque, site no. 63.)

It had been a long time coming, but the temple was finally dedicated on May 17, 1884. Its completion was a miracle—but not the only one.

HENRY'S
MIRACLE

Chapter Fifteen

In a way, Henry's life was one of miracles. He survived in his mother's womb despite her attempts to lose him. In his youth he survived the "Black Plague," and was healed by Mormon missionaries. On his trip up the Mississippi River, aboard the ill-fated steamboat Saluda, Henry narrowly escaped death when the boiler blew up and killed nearly 100 people. It was only a few weeks later when his party was struck by the dreaded cholera. The epidemic took most of the May family, including his beloved Elizabeth. Henry himself contracted the disease, but was again spared from death.

Henry, being a very private person, never tried to draw attention to himself. Surely he recognized the miracles in his life, but for reasons known only to himself, he chose to remain silent about the one we will examine here. An excellent account of it is found in the book, *Melvin J. Ballard, Crusader for Righteousness,* beginning on page 13. It was authored by Henry's grandson, Melvin R. Ballard, and is reproduced here with full permission of the family.

It was in the 1880's, when Henry and Margaret had been married about twenty-three years, that an event occurred which has become something of a classic among the many accounts of miracles in the Church—of divine intervention in the affairs of men.

About 1883, a writer vacationing in Berkshire, England, was led by fancy (or was it a higher inspiration?) to visit churches and churchyards and copy from the inscriptions on the monuments and headstones the "quaint verses" and other detail which struck him "as of general interest and worthy of preservation." The first visit made on this unusual vacation was to the ancient church at Thatcham—the birthplace, half a century before, of Henry Ballard. He later sent the notes of this visit with a prefatory paragraph or two, to the *Newbury Weekly News*, a newspaper founded in 1867, which published the items under the pseudonym "Wanderer."

No one took vacations in 1883 in Logan, Utah. That small city, only a little over twenty years old, hummed with industry and suppressed excitement as its temple neared completion. The Ballards had a big stake in the temple. Henry had hauled the first load of sand for construction in July 1877, a couple of months after the site was dedicated, and throughout the entire construction period he had worked long and faithfully on this labor of love. The whole family had made many sacrifices to further the work.

As well as temple building, temple work for the dead was a vital concern to Henry Ballard. Ever since arriving in Utah in 1852 he had diligently and anxiously sought information about his relatives in England, but apart from the knowledge that his three brothers had died he had learned almost nothing. As the dedication date for the temple drew near the family offered, with increased fervor, their oft-repeated supplication for the Lord's help in gaining information about his dead kindred. With such information they would be able to perform the saving Gospel ordinances for them in the temple now on their doorstep.

At last the day of dedication arrived—May 17, 1884. The temple was crowded to capacity as the venerable prophet, President John Taylor, led the sacred services and stirred all hearts with his dedicatory prayer. Recognizing the faith of the members in the area, and wishing to spread wider the sweet spirit of the services, President Taylor arranged for another dedicatory session on Sunday, the 18th, which all worthy members who so desired might attend.

The 18th found a line of members outside Bishop Henry Ballard's home as he wrote recommends for his ward members.[1] The day was warm and pleasant, and Ellen, Henry's nine-year-old daughter, was chatting with friends on the sidewalk outside the house when two elderly men approached, walking in the middle of the street. One of the men called, "Come here, little girl." As Ellen hesitated, the stranger pointed to her and said, "I mean you." Placing a newspaper in her hand, he said: "Take this to your father. Give it to no one else. Go quickly and don't lose it."

Henry's wife, Margaret, now picks up the story. "Ellen came in and asked for her father. I told her that her father was busy [writing recommends] and asked her to give me the newspaper she had in her hand so that I might give it to him. She said, 'No, the man who gave the paper to me told me to give it to no one but Father.' I let the child take the paper to her father."

Henry quickly took in the situation. The newspaper was the *Newbury Weekly News* containing "Wanderer's" jottings from Thatcham churchyard—names and other genealogical details for sixty or so now-dead acquaintances of Henry and his father. Who had brought it? Rapidly quizzing Ellen he hurried outside, went around the block searching and questioning. In that sparsely settled community, where all the inhabitants were known to each other, no neighbors had seen the two strangers. They were never found. This disappearance of the messengers was itself cause enough to wonder, but perhaps even more impressive was the date on the newspaper—May 15, 1884. In an era long before the advent of air transportation and when mail took several weeks to get from England to western America, this newspaper had made the journey in three days!

The next day Bishop Ballard took the newspaper and recited the facts to President Merrill, president of the Logan Temple, who concluded: "Brother Ballard, someone on the other side is anxious for their work to be done and they knew that you would do it if this paper got in your hands. It is for you to do the work, for you received the paper through messengers of the Lord." To their great joy, the Ballards received baptism

---

[1] See entries: May 18–19, p. 130.

and endowment in the temple for all the people he had listed. "Wanderer" never knew, in this life, the great work his vacation ramblings had made possible. Henry was then unaware of what subsequent generations have discovered— that some of the listed names link with Ballard family genealogy.

The Ballard family have always accepted with complete assurance that this incident occurred as recorded and that it reflects the hand of the Lord. Indeed, Henry's daughter, Rebecca Ballard Cardon, who was six when the event occurred, is alive today (1966) and recalls the circumstances clearly, as well as the local knowledge of the matter and the testimonies she heard in her mature years from people who were at the Ballard home when the newspaper was received. Rebecca's sister, Myrtle Ballard Shurtliff, has similar recollections. But sometimes rationalizers have tended to question—for instance, perhaps the newspaper was postdated. Consequently, the family made checks. Miracles cannot always be documented—but this one is. The following facts emerge in summary:

A representative of the family visited the office of the *Newbury Weekly News* in 1948, and saw and handled that office's copy of the issue of May 15, 1884. The entire issue was then photographed on the spot and a signed statement completed certifying that it was copied at its place of publication in England. Comparison reveals that the photographed copy is identical with the copy handed to Henry Ballard on May 18, 1884, which now rests in the Church Historian's Library in Salt Lake City.

At the 1948 interview the Publisher, Mr. Ashley Turner, affirmed to the family representative before several witnesses that the newspaper had never been postdated—it had always been printed on Wednesday night and distributed on Thursday morning of every week.

By official Somerset House records the family confirmed the death of a prominent citizen recorded on the same page as "Wanderer's" article, as May 8, 1884. Bells [that] rang in the parish church "last Sunday," as the death notice states, must have been rung on May 11, only seven days before the newspaper was delivered in Western America. The point is conclusive.

Small wonder that the newspaper, now yellowed and somewhat ragged with age, has always been regarded as a sacred treasure by the Ballard family.[1]

The "representative of the family" mentioned is Henry's great-grandson, Elder M. Russell Ballard, an Apostle of the Lord Jesus Christ. In a recent interview he recounted the event to the author.

> As a young man I was serving a mission in England for the LDS Church. At an appropriate time I asked the mission president for permission to go to the office of the *Newbury Weekly News*, telling him why it was important that I go. Permission was granted, and I soon found my way to the desk of Mr. Ashley Turner, then the publisher of the *Weekly*. I explained to him that I wanted to see the original copy of the May 15, 1884, issue of the paper. He offered a variety of reasons why he could not accommodate me, and was ready to dismiss me without granting my request.

> Saddened, but determined, I told him the story behind the reason for my request, and I then bore powerful testimony to him of the truthfulness of it. At that moment all of the aforementioned reasons seemed to melt away as he led me to the archives. The issue was located, and Mr. Turner allowed me to photograph it for my family and any other interested parties. What a thrill it was to be able to verify that which I already knew to be true!

Thank heaven for the persistence of a young missionary.

---

[1] According to his daughters this newspaper was held as a sacred gift, and as long as he lived Henry kept it folded and pressed between the pages of his temple record, under lock, in his desk. It was not talked of by him, except on rare occasions, to his own family.

31 Latimer Rd Notting Hill
London W July 16 1887

Dear Wife Margaret and children
I again take the pleasure of answer
-ing your kind and welcome letter
of th June 24 and was glad to hear
that you was all well and hope
that this will still find you all
in the enjoyment of good health
and spirits as thank God it have
me at present the weather has
been the dryest that England has
seen for a long time in some parts
the people are having to buy water
to drink I am glad to hear that the
Boys are getting along so well in
making their grain racks and hope
that they will have good luck with
the header and that the grain will
not be too badly srunk with the
dry weather that you have been
having but we will have to trust
in the Lord and do our duty

Henry's handwriting

HENRY'S
MISSION

Chapter Sixteen

Having recounted Henry's miracle, we will now return to his journal. The last previous entry was dated June 4, 1884—about two weeks after the Logan Temple opened for ordinance work.

No additional entries were noted until summer when his old enemy overtook him again in the last part of August, 1884:

> I was taken very sick in the feild with my old complaint[,] the gravel and pains in the Kidneys

Henry's mother, now eighty-six, died on September 14, 1884. She was buried in the Logan Cemetery on September 20. Her funeral was held in the Logan Tabernacle.

Henry William was now an elder. Henry ordained him on October 1.

> (Octr) 2   He got his Endowments and was married in the Temple to Elvira Davidson, Daughter of Bishop Robert Davidson of the Third Ward...

The new year, 1885, started with another addition to the family.

Jany 13 My wife Emiley bore me another Daughter[.] we named her Amey Eugine

On May 19, Henry notes:

My Father Died aged about 96 years of age

(May) 20   He was burried[.] the funerial services was also held in the Taberncacle[.] many old settler[s] of Logan was in attendance, it was a very unsettled time as the Deputy United marshel was on the track of every one living in Poligamy, I had to be away from home the most of my time, some of my freinds pursuaded me that I had better not attend the funeral in publick, but I told them it was the last thing that I could do for my father and I should attend [even] if I should get arrested, but I was not interupted

Henry's final note for 1885 is another happy one.

Aug 21   My Wife Margaret bore me another Daughter[.] we named her Mary Myrtle

Henry wrote little in 1886 as he was being hounded by the U.S. marshalls for his involvement in polygamy. The first entry he penned was dated simply "1886 Octr."

The most of this year I had to be away from home[.] The fore part of this month it became so hot with the Duputies on my tract till I had to come home to Logan in the night and hide up in some of the saints houses, and as soon as I had left my ranch where my Wife Emily and her familey was living in the summer seasons the Duputies came on the hunt for me, and as they could not find me they arrested her or rather supeaneded her to appear before the Grand Jury, and as the Judges had lately begun to try the segregation business upon the Bretheren, that is to make so many cases against a man what they claime for each offence, so by their infamous acts they could keep a man there in Prison for life, or at least for many years, but some time after this there was a test case made out involving apostle Lorenzo Snow in the case, as he was in the Utah Penitenuary serving out several segragation terms, it was brought before the United States supreme court at Washington and there decided that a man could not be tried for only one offence for the same thing[,] so many of the Bretheren was liberated from the Pen upon this discion [decision] of that the highest court in the Land[.] But as this was not found out till after I had made up my mind to get

140

away from this unjust percicution and take a Mission to England my native home and visit my relatives and gather geneoliges so I could do more good than spend the rest of my days in Prison[.] I therefore consulted with Apostle F. D. Richards about taking such a mission and his advice was for me to go at once, so I only had 2 Days to get ready before starting

Margaret played a significant part in this secret plan for Henry "to come home to Logan in the night and hide up in some of the saints houses," and her part should be noted here. Years later Margaret wrote:

To avoid capture my husband left home and went to Cache Junction. He would change his hiding places for deputies were out to find him.

While he was there I was praying to know what to do for the best. I felt that the Lord could save us more than anyone else. After I had gone to bed, thinking about it, I heard a voice say, "It is time he was moving from where he is." It was repeated again and I said "Where shall he go"?

The same voice replied, "Take him to Aunt Rosina Morrell's." I did not sleep any time that night but wrote a note telling my husband that I felt impressed that he should return home. If he decided to do so, I told him I felt that he should ride in a load of hay as far as the old slaughter house and cut across the fields and that I would meet him below on the railroad track. In the meantime I had made arrangements with Sister Morrell for him to stay with her.

That evening we saw each other for only a few minutes. He hurried through the back yards to Sister Morrell's where he stayed for three weeks.

As was mentioned by Henry, the officers came to the ranch the next morning after he had left Cache Junction. He didn't mention that they ran pitchforks in the wheat bins and haystacks to make sure he was not there.

The decision to go on a mission had been made, and the trick was to get out of town without being detected by the deputies. On Halloween night 1886, Henry, with Henry William's help:

...started after Dark going by team to Salt Lake City[.] my son Henry Wm taking his team...

Henry William remembered that night very well.

We drove all night in the worst storm I have ever seen. Wind was terrible and the rain and hail blinded us until we couldn't see the road. Thunder shook the earth and the lightning nearly blinded us. Then there was a heavy fall of snow. We had to trust our faithful horses to keep the road.

Earlier in the evening officers of the law lined the roads watching for the Polygamists. Father and his companion had shaved off their beards and disguised themselves as foreigners. The storm proved a blessing to us for the roads were now deserted and not a soul molested us. We drove all night to Bountiful without a stop. Here we stopped only long enough to eat breakfast and then drove on to Salt Lake.

Leaving was a difficult choice for Henry. He was nearly fifty-five years old, and he was leaving behind the two women he loved and his children—equally loved. While he was gone, each family had to provide for themselves, as Henry could not assist them.

This note, taken from Henry's journal, was dated and written on Halloween night; the same night Henry William drove him to Salt Lake City to depart for England.

...Now the rest of my Journal will be found in my other Book which I kept while upon my mission in England which will be always very intresting to me if not to any one else to read

Henry's journal, like many missionary journals, is filled with routine entries, most of which will not be addressed here. There are entries, however, that should be included because many readers will relate to them, especially older missionaries. Still other readers will be happy our more modern missionaries are generally spared some of these experiences. Lastly, family members need to know that Henry made contact with many of his relatives left behind when he sailed to America.

After being set apart by Franklin D. Richards[1] , Henry departed from Salt Lake City on the Denver and Rio Grande Railroad. The trip across the plains was familiar to him, but Niagara Falls and the Susquehanna River were not—nor was New York City.

Henry booked passage on the steamship *Alaska,* and he was on the high seas by November 12, 1886, when he wrote this comment:

I was taken very sick with my old complaint, the Gravel, and in much pain till after dark...

The *Alaska* docked at the port of Liverpool on November 17. The trip over the Atlantic Ocean had taken but nine days—much different from the ten weeks Henry spent coming to America thirty-five years earlier.

Henry had been ill on both trips, but on this trip he found himself so weakened physically that he was unable to walk to the Church office, and had to take a cab. Once there he was assigned to labor in the London Conference. The mission, at the time, consisted of several conferences.

After settling in Henry went right to work:

Dec 16   Went to Thatcham and visited my Nephew William's wife's parents, Mr. Joyce[,] and also the work shops that my brothers used to own but all having died a few years before. We then visited the old Church Yard where my Brothers and a number of old aquaintances lay. I gathered quite a few of their names with dates and then went to visit a Mr. Edward Pinnock, his wife was my Bro Charles Neice

---

[1] This was the second time Henry left Cache Valley for an extended period of time—the first being 1864 when he traveled east to help bring immigrants back to Utah. As bishop of the Second Ward, it must have been difficult to leave for he was not released from being bishop. However, when Henry was set apart by Franklin D. Richards, part of the blessing offered this comforting advice. "...Lay aside the cares of your Bishopric, leave them in the land of Zion, and go forth to your native land, the other sphere, and win Souls in the Church and labor to establish the fullness of the Gospel wherever you labor..."

[Niece] by his second marriage. We had a good comfortable bed and Bro Schofield [Henry's companion] remarked in the morning that it was too good for a Mormon Elder and told me to ask the woman how much our bill would be[,] but I told him that I did not think that they meant to charge any thing, but when I ask the man he refered me to his wife. When she ask me how much I thought it was worth I told her I had never paid for a bed yet for I had always been with friends so she finally charged us 2 shillings each for our Tea and breakfast so we had nothing to thank them for and they lost our blessing but we gave them tracts.

Dec 17   We visited my old home Cold Ash, where I left 35 years before on going to Utah, I visited the old house and sat down in it for an hour. It looked very much like it was when I left and I felt to thank God for the change and for my Mountain home and family and society of the saints in Zion.

Dec 20   I went again to Thatcham and found some more families and learned the where abouts of a cousin George Russell in Reading where I got a few names of my other relatives. In the evening we went to visit a man by the name of William Osgood who I had met on the road a few days before and [he] invited me to call at his house[,] and on doing so in the evening his wife met me at the door and would not admit me but told me her husband knew more than I did[,] thank God[,] and then slamed the door in my face. I bid her good night and returned back two miles feeling alright.

Henry, through persistence, was able to locate a good many of his relatives. He spent a lot of time with his nephew, George, the son of Henry's deceased brother of the same name. It was the older George who had driven Henry from his home many years before. He received some mail, took a few meals, and on occasion slept at George's home. The younger George seems to have had none of the animosities toward Henry that his father had harbored. On at least one occasion he even accompanied Henry to church. Other family members treated Henry well. Some of them even paid his train fare once in awhile.

Jan 19   I bid my nephew and family adue and started out to hunt new relatives. I went to Weybridge and found my aunt

Ann widow of George Ballard [not his brother] from Taplow
and my cousin Sarah Gillet wife of David Gillet who my aunt
was living with. They treated me very kindly,...

Jan 20 Remained with them and went around the place some
and got in conversation with the assistant gardiner that was
under her husband and also the coachman of his master[.] he
was very stupid to talk to on the Bible.

Jan 21 I bid them good bye my cousin paying for my ticket
to go on to my other cousin at Reigate and told me if I ever
needed money to let her know and she would help me.

Henry makes no mention of making any progress
toward the gospel with any of his relatives. It was nice just
to be welcome; however, he was not welcome everywhere.

Feb 15 Went againt to Cold Ash my native home and visited
at a farmer Mathews where his lady had invited me to call
when I had seen her one day before[,] but on arriving I found
a cold reception not asking me in at first and commenced on
me about Brigham Young and how many wives he had[.] I
told the lady that I was not out to tell how many wives he nor
my self had as she accused me of, neither did I wish to know
how many kept mistresses they had. She finally ask me into
the house when her big over grown son began telling me that
we all ought to be kicked out of the country....

Henry had been suffering from an infected foot, and all
of the walking he did was painful for him.

Feb 17 My foot was so swollen that I could not get my shoe
on and it was so fevered that it made me almost sick. It had
been poisoned with wearing red socks.

Mar 1 We left Newbury and went around by Midgam and
visited an old brother by the name of William Amer and then
called on Mrs Buckeridge at Theale and got tea and then
walked on to Reading, my foot was very sore we had walked
19 miles.

March 15 Still snowing, we bought a penny cake each and
started out walking and carring our satchels and holding our
umbrellas and our over coats on[,] and the snow pelting in our
face all the way and snow about 6 inches deep, we went
through old Windsor and Egham and Stains to Stanwell and
at last found a sister by the name of Charlotte Joy[,] and it

was a joy to us after walking 12 miles in such weather and
then find a warm fire and some dinner...we then walked on to
Ashford and took the train to London to my nephew George
Ballard.

Henry still hoped to convert some of his relatives, and
continued to seek them out.

Mar 19 I again called upon my Bro John's widow and also
my neices Sarah Ballard and Annie Ballard Daniels[.] her
husband was a minister and very bigoted and unbeleiving
denying near every thing of Gospel and a sign seeker. I was
with him for over 5 hours.

Henry communicated frequently with his families at
home, and many others. He also visited England's historical
sights, and other places of interest in the area, but mostly he
worked. His efforts did not go unnoticed.

At a priesthood meeting held on April 25, President
Teasdale, after a lengthy meeting, released the current
London Conference president and reassigned two elders to
other areas.

He then sat down saying that the Lord had not yet made it
known to him who should be the next President. Every thing
was quiet for five minutes. I with the rest were exercising our
faith and prayers that the Lord would direct his mind alright
in the matter when he seemed lifted to his feet and made the
motion that Henry Ballard be appointed President of the
Conference and I felt overcome after the motion was put and
carried unanimously[.] I was then called upon to state my
feelings[,] and [it was] with much difficulty that I could tell
my feelings...I said I felt like Moses when called to deliver
Isreal, I was slow of speech and [had] a stamering tougue, but
was willing to trust in the Lord and my brethren to aid me to
try and do my duty to the best of my ability. I then went back
to my nephews for the night.

Nephi Schofield, one of Henry's companions, was
present at that meeting and recalled it years afterward.

We sat as if in a Quaker meeting, speechless, but all
exercising our faith for Brother Teasdale to choose the right
man. We were almost overcome by a cloud which produced
an atmosphere of great oppressiveness. President Teasdale sat

looking at us all and then suddenly with great vigor, as though he was lifted by an unseen power, he jumped to this feet and said, "It is the will of the Lord that Brother Henry Ballard be appointed to fill this office." At this announcement Brother Ballard nearly collapsed in his seat, and when he was called to respond he was almost speechless. Revelation has been restored for truly I have witnessed a revelation. This was a revelation from God.

Returning to Henry's journal:

April 26 I took my things and returned to the office.

Henry was now officially at the helm of the London Conference.

Street meetings were common among proselyters in the late eighteen hundreds. The Mormon missionaries in the London Conference had their share of street meetings, but there were occasional problems.

Henry never felt comfortable speaking at a street meeting and avoided it, if possible. As conference president he relegated the job to the missionaries. However, he hated asking them to do anything that he didn't do. Henry spent a lot of time fasting and praying for strength to overcome the weakness he felt. At times he would eat only one meal a day for weeks. Henry had the ability to speak, and spoke for long periods at almost every meeting he attended. He felt perfectly at ease in this situation. Street meetings were another matter to him. True to his character, Henry made up his mind to correct this area of his behavior. Again, we rely on Brother Nephi Schofield to describe how Henry conquered his fear.

The meeting was held on Portaballa Road. Brother Ballard had experienced a great fear and dread of speaking at a street meeting and had felt that Satan had been holding him from bearing his testimony, and because of this feeling he had not made an effort. He finally felt determined to do so. He apologized to the Elders for not doing what he had ask them to do. He ask the Elders to pray for him and to use their faith in his behalf. He had fasted every day, with but one meal a day for three weeks, to overcome his weakness. His companion was the first speaker and spoke for a short time and then with a very timid voice Brother Ballard started to speak. His voice did not carry well, and the clattering of the horses hoofs over the noisy cobble road during the heavy traffic, drowned [out] his voice completely, and Brother Ballard gained little attention. All at once his voice broke and he became possessed with an unusual voice, deep and loud, and the people all around immediately turned to see what was up, and the travelers on the bus stood up to see what was going on. His voice was as loud as a fog horn on a steamer, and sounded above all the noise of the street. A man in the corner store could not hear what customers ask for because of his speaking. A large crowd soon gathered and the police ask them to move on for they were blockading the traffic. On every successive occasion Brother Ballard began to speak in a low meek modest way and invariably his voice would break into loud thunderous tones as he proceeded in his speaking[,] and at no other time would this happen—only at the street meetings. Surely he was a son of thunder.

Henry had indeed mastered his weakness and spoke at many more outdoor meetings. Most went very well, but some did not.

July 14 ...The Brethren again had opposition at their out door meeting[.] I was not with them again.

Henry's presence, however, didn't necessarily insure success. Consider his August 23 description of a street meeting.

Bro Morris and myself went to the Harrow Road and held a meeting on that road[.] I commenced to speak and very soon gathered a large crowd and they listened for a while when a drunken woman came up and stood before me and commenced to talk as loud as she could to break up the meeting and others joined in with her[,] but I talked to the top of my voice to drown hers untill I had talked 30 or 40 minutes[,] and had gathered a large crowd of over 300 and the rable got too bad to continue any longer[.] many of the more sensible portion was sorry to see how the others acted[.] they took all the tracts we had and wanted more and we gave out about 100[.] as soon as I stopped a crowd gathered around Bro Morris with a mob like feeling and I could not get to him nor him to me till I cried out for them to make a circle larger so we could all hear him[,] and they broke back a little so I could crowd my way to reach him with my arm and called him to come on and broke the road for him when I lost him again and I was surrounded with them and he got me out[.] they threatened us but I told them I did not fear any of them[.] I had given them a testimony that would stand against them and they could please themselves wether they received it. I had borne my testimony to the devine mission of Joseph Smith before they had drowned my voice and through the blessings of the Lord we got away from them all safe but they did not intend for us to get away so safe[.] several ladies begged of me to get Bro Morris out of the crowd that he was surrounded with for fear of danger.

A man named Jarman[1] was an anti-Mormon group leader. His groups were present and well organized in the London Conference at that time. Henry met them face to face on September 10, 1887.

...Between the meetings some of Jarman's followers came along the street with their printed libellous sheets againts us. Bro's Cannon and Lusty went out to them to try and reason with them till they had gathered quite a crowd, I then went out and listened to him telling the people that the people could not leave Utah without endangering their lives and this was a little more than I could stand and I stepped up to him and told him that he was a Damn liar and I could prove it. I felt ashamed that I had been so plain with him[,] but could not help it for he was so full of lies[.] Jarman had sent his [hand] bills calling the people to come to Hamersmith near where he was going to expose the Mormons by his ludicours pictures and his costume of Temple clothing.

Two days later:

Sep 12 ...Bro's Morris and Schofield went to see Jarmans show and it was wicked and full of the devil. He berated us and told the people where we were stopping.

At the end of September, almost a year into his mission, Henry was still calling on his relatives to present

---

[1] Jarman was eventually committed to Hamwell Asylum in Middlesex, England.

the gospel plan to them. The following entry must have been written with a little bit of sadness in his heart.

> Sept 27 ...in the Evening I went to Wansworth and visited my cousin Sophia Chapman and my second cousin Jerimiah August living with her. They did not care to listen to the Gospel.

The Jarman movement continued to escalate. It soon became so abusive and intolerable that Henry was forced to move the office of the London Conference to a new address. Henry described it this way:

> Oct 2 ...Bro Burningham returned with me to the office to hold the West London meeting and when we got back we found that Jarman had been having his men parading the streets with big hand bills against us carring them on a board creating an excitement and he held a meeting near by us and a part of them come and rushed up stairs and filled our little room packing it full and nearly 500 out on the street, I commenced to talk but at times I could not keep them quiet but I talked to them for 45 minutes[,] at times very quiet[,] but they commenced to climb upon one anothers shoulders and get in at the [second story] window and before the police came onto the ground they broke down the iron railing and brick work on front of the house damaging about four pounds[1] of which we had to pay one half[.] they also did some damage in the house, the police kept them back from doing any further damage. In the evening they came back but finding no meeting the police kept them back and none of us got hurt, the LandLord gave us notice to vacate the house within a week as he said the mob would tare his house down.

The first year had been an exciting one for Henry, and ended with the following note:

> Oct 31 It was just one year since I left my home. I got a letter from home telling me that my littler girl Myrtle had been again very sick but was now again much better.

At about the halfway point in his mission, Henry was prompted to write the following in a letter to home:

---

[1] Pounds sterling (£)—the British money system.

...the work of the Gospel is a grand work and we feel proud to be connected with it. I pray that we may always feel humble and do our duty in the Kingdom of God[,] and O what joy when we have overcome and gained the victory.

In another letter Henry profoundly stated:

...I hope that we may all have strength to endure the trials of life for we are very often a trial to each other.

Journal entries over the next few months refer often to Jarman and his henchmen. Henry finally took one of them to court and obtained a restraining order, but the confrontations still continued. The best approach, it seemed, was to return their mail unopened, and try to ignore them. Of this group no more need be said; however, there were other detractors.

Christmas day, 1887, was enjoyable for Henry. He spent it with his nephew George and his family.

Imagine the flood of memories that must have filled Henry's mind as he penned this entry:

Jan 22 Sunday...I visited the London News London St Tottenham Court Rd where I had once lived with my brother George and turned out of doors by him in the Spring of 1851 because I would not forsake Mormonism but he died in 1864 but I attended to the work in the Temple for him[1]

His heart must have filled with despair as he pondered these lines.

Mar 15 ...I then called at my niece Annie Daniels the Minister's wife and found my Bro Johns widow there[.] they expressed a feeling of hatred toward me and did not want me [there] but could not but treat me decent[,] but did not ask me to eat anything...She refered to the discussion between me and her husband and she thought he was right but I was wrong, I told her she would learn better some day,...I returned back to the office feeling that I had but very few friends

---

[1] One of the first endowments Henry performed after the dedication of the Logan Temple was for his brother George—June 5, 1884. Two weeks later George was sealed to his father and mother.

among my relatives and I would have to wait till they died before I could benefit them any for they would not harken to my testimony

It was the same on March 23.

...I then hunted up a young woman by the name of Elizabeth Mason who had a mother in Utah that had asked me to find her daughter[,] but after I had walked a long distance I found her so bitter that she did not want to speak to me as she said her mother had left a blind husband and 5 children behind, but I tried to reason with her but without effect, and she shut the door on me

Henry was not the only one with problems.

April 5 I walked both ways making 6 miles, on the road going I met a respectable woman who stopped me, and commenced telling me her troubles and her want, she seemed to be telling the truth, I gave her a penny to buy her a cake with.

During his mission Henry was often plagued with sickness. There are numerous entries concerning his infected foot, but usually it was his "old complaint, the gravel," meaning kidney stones. These few entries are typical of the many that reflect this malady.

April 10 I visited Bro Gladwins in the evening but I felt sick and had to return to the office early and was quite sick all night with the pain in my kidneys again. I rested very little.

April 11 I still felt very sick but tried to keep up but the pain was very acute[.] between times I got the Brethren to administer to me in the afternoon an I felt some better.

April 12...I was so distressed with the pain at night that I got Bro Schofield to administer to me again and I rested a little better a portion of the night.

April 13 I felt a little easier the forepart of the day but worse again in the afternoon until about 11 in the night when the pain left me and I slept good the first for four nights.

Of course, there were some successes as well.

April 27 ...in the evening sister Emily Robinson the young woman that I baptized came to the office to visit us for a short time[,] she was feeling well in the gospel...

If one were to add up all the time Henry notes he talked in meetings, it would be hundreds of hours. Usually he felt like the Spirit was with him and modestly pointed that out. Some of the meetings were to large congregations, as many as 1,500 souls, and other groups were very small. Henry addressed all of them. Often he spoke several times a day, and sometimes people listened.

> May 6 Sunday ...I took up all the time in the evening[,] about 70 minutes to a good sized congregation[.] The Lord blessed me in my testimony. Sister Hull came with me to Mrs Donoghue and four other strangers some of which was well satisfied.

Another time he notes:

> ...I spoke for 45 minutes and the Lord blessed me with great freedom...

Still later:

> ...we had 4 non members at our meeting on Mile End[.] I spoke first for 30 minutes and Bro Leiang followed for 40 minutes but an old opponent came and opposed us which brought quite a crowd[,] at least 400[,] but the Elders bore them powerful testimonies and I steped out and told them I would close with prayer when the spirit of the Lord came upon me in such power that I stood forth in the fear of God and bore my testimony in the voice of thunder to that crowd that gave me good attention[.] I then closed with prayer[.] I felt that good had come from intended evil.

Good did come of it.

> I met a young lady at Bro Pyes by the name of Miss Beal who had attended our meetings and had requested baptism but I appointed to meet her there to teach her further of our doctrines and see if she understood what she was doing and I was very pleased to learn that she was fully prepared for baptism.

> ...in the evening we had 8 new members and some never had been to meeting before[.] I spoke one hour[.] I felt very good, at the close 3 women gave in their names for baptism...

Henry's next entry is rather interesting.

Aug 2 ...while I was speaking a man began to oppose me and several tried to get him to keep still but he tried to get me to stop but I took but little notice of him, he finally went around behind me and Bro Wadsworth thought he was going to give me a blow [and] he came close up to defend me, but right then a lad told him to shut up and that annoyed him, so he then struck at the lad but another young man took him a blow on the head and then ran off and him after him so the Lord protected us and we had a good meeting[.] I spoke 25 minutes.

Aug 27 ...in the evening we went onto the Kilburn Rd and held a meeting[,] we had nearly 200 to listen a part of the time, 3 of the Brethren spoke taking up about 60 minutes, the last one had considerable opposition, I steped into the circle and told them I was born and raised among them and returned of my free will, and I wanted them to look at me and listen for a few minutes, the Lord blessed me to speak to them for 15 minutes till they were all quiet and listened very attentive[.] I then closed with prayer.

Nov 17 ...It was just 2 years since I landed in Liverpool.

Nov 20 I visited Bro Robinson and called upon Mrs Enderson but they were not yet ready for baptism, in fact they were not yet a fit subject for it, I then went on to Wallaces and had quite a talk with him in regard to this faith in the gospel, and I found he had none, and he said it was a deception and would send in his request to be cut off the church[.] I told him I thought it was about time if he had been so deceived.

Dec 3 ...with our labors we had baptized 54 during the year and emigrated 70 and still about 600 members in the conference

Henry's mission was quickly drawing to a close.

Dec 18 I got a letter from Pres Teasdale stating that he had received a letter from the Presidency in Salt Lake City dated Nov 28 stating that I should be released to return home at an early date

Then, quoting President Teasdale, Henry wrote:

While I am sorry to loose your valuable assistance I rejoice in your release to go home to your family, I feel persuaded you will prosper and enjoy the Blessings of Almighty God for your faithful labor, and the report of your earnest labors will be sent to the Presidents office, I am sure you will leave with the faith, prayers and blessings of all the saints who know you, who will remember your fatherly counsels and earnest testimony for the truth, you will see the effect of the seed sown, to your perfect satisfaction, with best wishes from all at 42 Islington by George Teasdale.

Returning to Henry:

This was a part of the Kind letter from my beloved President which filled my heart with joy to overflowing.

Dec 23 ...after meeting Bro Leiang presented me as a token of respect from the Elders from Utah a very nice warm Rug or Blanket to keep me warm while traveling home[,] also made a very kind and touching speech and asking Gods blessings upon me which I very much appreciated and [I] made a short speech for their kindness to me[.] I then wished the saints good bye which I did not expect to see again...

Dec 25 "Christmas Day" I spent it with my Nephew George Ballard where I had spent two before I had a very agreeable time with them and wished them good bye for the last time.

Dec 27 Was closing up the books...I had spoken at 212 meetings in the Halls and also spoken at 32 out door meetings while I have been upon my mission.

Dec 28 ...I left at 10:10 A. M. feeling satisfied with my labors that I had done the best I could and had made many warm friends and gained the fellowship of the Elders and saints long to be remembered by me[.] I arrived at Liverpool at 2:30 P.M....In the evening I took a walk with Pres Teasdale and had quite a chat with him, he was well satisfied with my labors in the conference.

Dec 29 ...started on board the steam ship "Wisconsin"... located in a small room for our births [berths] all to ourselves in the cabin and eating at the same table with the captain and Purser and Doctor.

Dec 30 ...I took a light breakfast...but I soon threw it all up

Dec 31 Was still very sick, I got up and washed but had to lay down again, and could keep nothing upon my stomach but a few grapes and an apple.

Jan 1, 1889 Was getting worse sick as the sea was getting very rough...

Jan 2 ...[Bro Woods and I] were both very sick

Jan 3   The sea was so rough it broke in 3 portholes and tons of water rolled over the wheel house...

Jan 6   Sunday was a very fine morning the ship making 260 miles in 24 hours consuming 70 tons of coal during the time. I felt quite well and ate a hearty breakfast...the Captain held church of England service in the Saloon but no sermon, I felt like I would liked to have preached it for him but did not deem it wise to ask for the priviligege...but I thought what a difference to that of the Saviour's teaching...

On December 9, the ships purser,[1] by tradition, held a lottery costing 2 shillings for each ticket holder. The winner would be whoever drew the number of the pilot boat that ushered them into the harbor. The boat was number nine— the number Henry had selected. He had won the 30-shilling lottery. Of this he said:

...after I paid the Purser my own and Bro Woods back, I felt [it] was a gift from God

Maybe it was a gift from God. Henry didn't even have the money to pay in advance.

Henry chose to go on a mission, but only out of desperation dictated by his unusual circumstances. No doubt he would have preferred to remain at home with his families. But in retrospect, Henry probably would have said, like all other missionaries, "It was the best two years of my life." His final entry in his missionary journal reads:

Jan 16 ...I took the freight train to Logan at 11 P.M.

Henry left in the dark of night, and he returned in the dark of night. The train carried him over the same tracks he had helped to lay fifteen years earlier. He also returned to the persecution he had left two years earlier.

---

[1] Financial officer.

FROM PRISON
TO THE MANIFESTO

Chapter Seventeen

The next morning, January 17, 1889, the train pulled into Logan at 5:00 A.M. Henry was met at the station by his son Thomas. Finding all well at home he confined himself to his house trying to decide what to do next.

> Jan 19 Was writing letters to quite a few and remained in the house till I could find out what was best to be done, and all that I could learn was for me to give myself up for trial

Henry surrendered to the authorities on January 29, 1889, and was "bound over"[1] for the sum of $1,500 for himself and an additional $200 for Emily. On February 8, 1889, he was sentenced to two months' imprisonment plus court costs, which amounted to $38.50. The $38.50 was loaned to him by a Brother Dalton, and at eight o'clock that night:

> ...I was placed in cell no. 25, with Mark Hall from Ogden

The next day Henry noted:

> Feb 9 When we were turned out in the yard I found quite a number of Brethren that I knew, they were all enjoying

---

[1] Held for sentencing

157

themselves as best they could under the circumstances which was very comfortable for prison life, the most of them had striped clothes on except those who had short terms[.] I was not allowed any but I had to have my beard cut off

Henry was in good company. Apostle George Q. Cannon was among those serving time for "unlawful cohabitation," and based on Henry's brief entries, it appears that Apostle F. M. Lyman and Bishop William Maughan, of Wellsville, may also have served time with him.

Brothers Cannon, Lyman, and Maughan each conducted Sunday services for the Mormons held there. Ministers from other faiths also held services. On the Sundays Henry was on "pump duty," he hired another prisoner to do the work for him so he could attend the meetings.

Henry was visited quite frequently—he was thrilled when President Wilford Woodruff came to them—but the real highlight came on April 8. Henry noted:

My time came for my release and I bid farewell to my Brethern[.] My son Melvin came with the buggie to take me to the City...

The same entry contains less welcome news. Henry continues:

I there got a letter from home stateing that my children were sick with scarlet fever also my grand daughter was also very sick also my wife Margaret. I learned that a special train would go to Logan that night as the [General] Conference would close. I attended the last meeting[.] Bro W Woodruff had been sustained at the Conference as President of the Church...as I was just taking the train I received a telegram from home stateing that my little granddaughter Ada had died at 1 A.M. that morning. I arrived home at 11 P.M. and found my wife still sick also my little girl Amy very low.

April 30 ...A concert was held in the ward meeting house by the Primary to welcome me home[.] it was very good

Henry felt his surrender and term in prison would pay his debt to society and give him his freedom. Such was not the case. He was arrested several times for being seen with his daughter-in-law. Someone unwittingly assumed she was his wife Emily—so the persecution continued.

> Aug 24 I was again arrested for unlawful "cohab" by Dep Marshalls Pratt, Westone and Bowman, also my wives and their mother were subpenaed as witness. I had an examination before commissioner C C Goodwin[.] he failed to prove any thing against me but held me over for further witnesses to be brought against me

> May 31 [1890] Was again brought before the commissioners[.] Mrs Sarah Birdno [Birdneau] Card and her daughter Jennie testified that they saw me riding in a wagon with my wife Margaret[,] also Emily[,] but they were mistaken for I proved that it was my sons wife Elvira and my first wife in the wagon with me[.] I was then discharged by the court

Henry mentions little more about confrontations with the law concerning plural marriage; however, accusations and ill feelings toward the Church and its members continued for years.

Henry traveled to Salt Lake City to attend the October conference. Here he witnessed the appointment of another Apostle from Logan, Marriner W. Merrill, the Logan Temple president at the time. He also met Saints from the London Conference, along with several missionaries who served with him in London.

He baptized his little girl Jennie Lulu on October 22. The next event Henry recorded is of a tragic nature, but one very familiar to the Ballards.

> Dec 7 My daughter Ellen Pheobe was taken sick with a bad cold which set into Membranous croup[.] She continued to suffer with it, she was administered to many times[,] also was prayed for in the Temple but in the providences of the Lord she was destined to leave us.

> Dec 12 At 9 A.M. she died very peacefully aged 14 years and nearly 3 months, she was a lovely girl and kind to all, full of faith in the gospel and much devoted to the Sabbath school also to her studies in the B Y College and to her primary association.

Dec 14 We held her funeral in the 2nd ward meeting house[.] it was nearly full...each [speaker] made very comforting remarks calcuated to comfort us in our breavement, 18 carriages and wagons went to the grave yard.

Year's end found the Saints very concerned about religious persecution.

Dec 23 As it was the Prophet Joseph Smiths birthday it was decided by the first Presidency to call a general fast day to fast to commence at sundown on the 22nd and continue till the 23rd at sundown to seek the Lord in our behalf as a people[,] that he would soften the hearts of the law makers of our nation toward us so that we may possess our rights as free citizens of our great republic,...I met with the Brethren of the 2nd and 4th Wards in the morning in Prayer Circle[.] we had 26 present, I was mouth, we felt well. I then met with the saints of my Ward at 10 A.M. and 2 P.M. I took up a collection for the poor to buy them some coal[.] all responded very liberally, and we felt that our prayers would be remembered by the Lord.

On January 7, 1890, Henry was in the temple doing work for his kindred dead. Margaret and his daughter Rebecca were with him.

It was a hard winter. Henry noted that the snow "was about 2 1/2 feet on the level in the valley," and it created a few problems.

Jan 22 President M W Merrill of the Temple told us that he was afraid that they would be compelled to close the Temple for the want of coal as the trains were blockaded, but a train got through and a little coal was got so they could continue work. It was very hard to get any coal and nearly every body was out[,] and wood could not be got at any price[,] and much sickness with bad colds and fever.

It appears the Lord had not yet answered the Saints prayers about religious persecution.

Feb 2 ...a Telegram came stating that the supreme court of the U S had decided that the test oath gotten up in Idaho to deprive all Mormons from voting was legal, so it will rob all that believed in Mormonism from voting or holding any office.

Feb 10 Salt Lake City was robbed in their election by the coruption of the voting of the so called Liberals.

Henry's family was growing up. On February 15th, two of his sons were ordained—Willard to the office of priest, and Ernest of the office of deacon. Thomas was ordained to the office of elder on March 30. Three days later Thomas married Phoebe John Smith in the Logan Temple.

Summer passed without comment, but later Henry noted the following:

Sept 7 We had a very strong frost killing a good deal of vegetation, my crop at the ranch was very light, the rail road going through it[,] which cut it up very much, the station was built making the Junction upon my land.

Nov 30 I commenced hauling lumber to the ranch to build a Boarding house close by the Station[,] my wife Emily living there and attending to it. It was built of lumber at a cost of nearly $900.00.[1]

Dec 24 They moved into it but not yet finished

Dec 29 I went down to finish rocking up the well.

As the new year rang in, Henry was ill and unable to get out-of-doors for a few days. As a result of his illness tithing settlement was put off until:

Jan.14 [1891] I was able to get out of doors again, and begun settling Tithing with the people of the Ward.

On February 3, Henry was blessed with a new granddaughter. On February 9, Margaret and Emily's father, Thomas McNeil, passed away.

Henry also noted:

...there was a great deal of sickness among the people, in almost every family.

---

[1] The $900 was borrowed from Emily's brother, Hyrum.

161

Following in the footsteps of his father, Henry's oldest son was given a significant church calling.

> March 8 My son Henry William was called to be Bishop of Benson Ward, and was ordained a High Priest and set apart the next day by Apostle Moses Thatcher in Logan.

Thirty years as bishop had passed when Henry penned the following:

> April 14 A committee of Brethren and sisters went to work and got up a reunion of the Ward of all members in the Church[,] and out of all over 16 years of age, by giving a splended supper and presented me with a splended gold watch as a token of respect of the good feeling of the people on the aniversary of my Thirtieth year of my Bishoprick of the Ward, we had a good time. Apostle Moses Thatcher and the Presidency of the stake and Pres C O Card of Canada were in attendance together with the most of the Ward. The next day the children had their day of enjoyment with a dance.

Henry remained silent after his thirtieth-year anniversary until the following November.

> Nov 1 Our Quarterly conference commenced. Pres Woodruff also Geo Q Cannon and Jos F Smith who had just been pardoned a few weeks before by the Prest of the U. S. after being in exile for over seven years it was a treat to have them again in our midst. They spoke at length upon the Manifesto[1] that was presented to the saints at the conference in Salt Lake City last April setting forth that it was the will of the Lord that Polygamy should cease among this people for this nation was determined to disfranchise every Mormon and close our Temples if it was not stopped.[2] Pres Woodruff dedicated our Stake Tabernacle, they made it very plain that there were but two Priesthoods and all the difference there

---

[1] For the full text of the manifesto see Official Declaration–1, found in the Doctrine and Covenants on pages 291–92.

[2] This address by Wilford Woodruff was important not only to Henry but to all members of the Church everywhere. Excerpts of it have since become part of LDS scriptures, and can be found in the Doctrine & Covenants on pages 292–93.

was in each was the calling to fill different positions. We had many good instructions they were satisfied with the saints.

The balance of Henry's notes for the year talk of routine changes in the ward, visitors from London, Melvin J. Ballard's ordination to the office of priest, and his final entry is about the weather.

Dec 30 Was a very snowy day it fell nearly a foot deep[.] we had had very cold stormy weather the most of the month.

It had been a difficult three years for Henry and his family. The persecution he had tried so hard to avoid had, like a mongrel dog, followed him home.

The manifesto, now church doctrine, made it unlawful to practice polygamy. It did not, however, alter the fact that Henry had two wives and two families to sustain.

One way or another, life went on.

CAPSTONE AND
TEMPLE DEDICATION

Chapter Eighteen

The first significant entry for the year 1892 was on February 23.

> I went to Ogden to settle up a sale of land at my place at Cache Junction to Mr. F J Keisel, returning the same day.

Henry had mentioned the subject of politics on past occasions, but never declared his party—until now.

> Feb 24 I attended a convention of the Democratic party in the court house for officers to be elected for the City of Logan, a great deal of ill feeling had been gotten up with both parties which was not becoming to Latter-Day Saints.

> Mar 6 Sunday evening I spoke in my ward meeting asking the Brethren to be fair toward each other at the election the following day [,] and repuadiated the hard speeches which had been indulged in at times[,] and as I had not taken any hand in either party, only my feelings run with the Democrats but never made it known by using any infulence for that party, yet at the close of the meeting I was viloently assailed by two of my Brethren, C. W. Nibley and H. C. Peterson[,] leaders of the Republicans in my Ward[,] for what I had said.

> March 7 The republicans gained the victory at the poles by much scheming and all the Liberals who is the apostate element joining them

On March 17, Henry commented on the fifty-year anniversary of the "Female Relief Society" and of the various meetings held in response to the anniversary.

April 2, 1892, Henry, Margaret, and their daughter Rebecca traveled to Salt Lake City to attend the spring conference. It was to be a special conference in that the Church leaders planned to set the capstone on the Salt Lake Temple on April 6. Every worthy church member wanted to witness the event—Henry was no exception.

Henry didn't miss a single session, and he detailed the remarks of every speaker. While all of the remarks are worth repeating, only some of them will be presented here.

April 3 The conference commenced[.] It was very snowy and stormy weather for 3 days[,] yet the large Tabernacle was full at the first meeting on Sunday morning and in the afternoon the assembly hall was full and over flowing. Geo Q Cannon made the opening remarks encouraging the saints for the prospects before us, said that much ill feeling that had existed against us from our own nation was removed[,] also the same ill feeling from other parts of the world was also being removed, and the way for the spread of the gospel in various parts where it had been hindered before was being now opened up.... F D Richards spoke upon the necessity of continued revelation to lead the people. Heber J Grant urged the necessity of calling upon the Lord that we may keep that living witness and testimony and be united.... John W Taylor compared the course of the Latter Day Saints to that of a train engineer traveling in the dark, if he did not keep his eye steadily upon the light which reflected upon the road before his engine he was liable to wreck his train, so with every Latter Day Saint if he did not look well to his ways he was liable to become a wreck...

April 4 Monday Lorenzo Snow said the saints should know for themselves that this work was true and of God. Moses Thatcher spoke very spiritedly upon the necessity of us doing our duty in spreading an influence for peace and not of strife and while the changed condition of politics which we had been thrown into we must not sell our birthright for a mess of pottage...he wished that some of the Brethren [who] had been so intrested in politics...would be as much intrested in the work of God. In the afternoon G Q Cannon spoke very ernestly upon the position of us as a people with regard to politics, said many hard things had been said by both parties which pained him and we should now call a halt, and testified that the First Presidency had given no council which side the people should join themselves to, and if we did not stop our strife it would grieve the spirit of God...Pres Woodruff testified to the truth of the words of Bro Cannon...neither had he authorized any other person to persuade the people either way, and he had been pained by the course that some of the Twelve and other leading Elders had taken. J F Smith...said we should spare Pres Woodruff much of the family troubles for us as a people and take our troubles to our Bishops and Presidents of Stakes where it belonged....

April 5 ...John H Smith...ask the people to donate to the erection of a monument to Pres Brigham Young.[1] M W Merrill bore testimony that the servants of God that had passed away was intrested in our labors for the dead and that some had visited the Logan Temple where he was laboring namely, Heber C Kimball....George Q Cannon explained himself upon a remark that he made the day before wherein he said that J H Smith had only done what he had been told to do with regard to politics. He wished to say that J H Smith came to the Presidency and told them that he was a Republican and he wanted to advocate their principles[.] he was told that he was free like every other man to do so if he wanted to....The authorities of the Church was sustained that day.

April 6 All of the Priesthood took their appointed positions in the Tabernacle and all the rest of the people took seats in the galleries preparatory to the cerimonies of laying the cap stone of the Salt Lake Temple. Pres of the Quorum of the Twelve, Lorenzo Snow trained us, We shouted waiving our hankerchiefs Hosannah, Hosannah, Hosannah, then staying our hankerchiefs and shouting To God and the Lamb, then shouting with waiving hankerchiefs Amen, Amen, Amen, saying it all over three times. We all marched out into the Temple block, but such a large crowd it was hard to keep in the desired positions. Pres Woodruff stated the object of our

---

[1] The monument was built. It eventually came to rest at its present location—Main Street—just north of South Temple Street, in Salt Lake City.

gathering and said that it was 39 years since Pres Brigham Young layed the cornerstone and hoped to live to see this Temple finished and dedicated, at noon Pres Woodruff touched a button [to] which Electricity was applied[,] to raise the cap stone and then lower it into its proper position, after which the shouting and waiving was again gone through with as before, it was a grand time long to be remembered, it was estimated that there were about fifty or sixty thousand people upon the Temple block besides the great crowds upon the roofs of the houses and upon the streets, and the storms had cleared away and it was every thing that we could desire, a vote was taken by the people to donate sufficent means to finish it by next April so it could be dedicated at its fortieth year in building. F M Lyman offered $1000.00 as a donation for that purpose. In the afternoon the statue upon the pinnacle of the Temple was unveiled representing the Angel Moroni blowing a trumpet which was five feet long and the angel standing 12 1/2 feet[,] over laid with leaf gold.

April 7 ...took the train at 3:30 P.M. and went to Cache Junction where my other part of my family was living.

May 1 A general fast day of the whole church was called to give thanks unto the Lord for His kind mercies toward us in restraining our enemies and softening the feelings of the rulers of the nation toward us and asking Him to still give us more liberties; also take up a general free will offering to complete the Salt Lake Temple,...we had a testimoney and Prayer Meeting which lasted four hours, including taking up the Temple donation which was very liberal making over $800.00 at one meeting.

Conferences, whether a general conference in Salt Lake City, or a quarterly stake conference in Logan, were a large part of Henry's life. During his later years, much of his journal is devoted to recording them. It seems appropriate to include messages that reflect pioneer life, trends in the church, or Henry's life. Others are quoted merely to remind us that many of today's problems were also yesterday's problems, and they help us come to know that the more things change the more they remain the same. Many messages, equally important in the broader sense, have been omitted.

On May 8–9 a two-day stake conference in Logan was almost exclusively devoted to teaching Church doctrine, and Henry

> ...[thought] it to be one of the best conferences that we had had for a long time.

Henry again alludes to things political when on May 14 he notes:

> I went to Ogden as I had been Elected a Delegate together with 41 other Democrats from Cache County to attend a convention of that political party in Ogden to elect 2 delegates and 2 alternates to the convention to be held in Chicago on the 24th of June, we reached there by train at 10:30 A.M. and paraded the streets from the station to main street headed by the Logan band of which my son Melvin was the drummer....My son Henry William was also one of the Delegates. It was a great day for Ogden and the Territory at large, as the Delegates came from all parts.

Accidents were still a part of pioneer life. This time it was not Henry who was injured.

> June 21 My son Henry William got hurt at Benson Ward[.] a horse run away coming up from behind him while he was driving his team on foot without his wagon[,] and as he looked around the horse struck him in the face with the iron of the harness and broke his cheek bone and brused him up a good deal[.] they brought him home to my home in Logan and got doctor Parkinson to set the bone and made him feel as comfortable as possible. He soon commenced to get better.

Only three entries remain in Henry's notes for the rest of the year, and they deal with three separate subjects—all dear to him.

> Oct 30 Our Quarterly Conference commenced. J F Smith, Lorenzo Snow [and] J H Smith were here from the city. Bro Snow urged the saints to prepare themselves for the Dedication of the Salt Lake Temple next April...

> Nov 8 Was the Presidential election throughout the United States, the Republicans trying hard to get their man Benj. Harrison in, while the Democrats tried hard to get their

choice in Grover Cleveland but the great Democratic leader Grover Cleveland got an over whelming majority through Utah and the United States.

Dec 25 All of the family spent the Christmas at Cache Junction, we had a good family gathering and had a good time, although it was raining hard all the time, it took all the frost out of the ground[.] my son Thomas plowed some after Christmas

New Year's Day, 1893, fell on Sunday. A meeting was held in the tabernacle, and Apostle Moses Thatcher presented a discourse on the order of the priesthood. Like Apostle Marriner W. Merrill, Moses Thatcher was from Logan. With two Apostles from the area it was common for the Logan Saints to have an Apostle speak at their meetings.

Henry's sixty-first birthday was on January 27, 1893, and the raining and the thaw from Christmas still continued. He also noted his family had nearly all been ill, at one time or another, during the winter, and that a good many deaths had occurred among the Saints throughout the valley. The balance of the winter of 1893 was consumed in sickness, quarterly stake conference, ward conference, and the normal day-to-day activities expected of Church members, including:

a Bishops Court in the Ward between Logan Cow pasture Co and John Davidson.

By the end of March thoughts turned toward the forthcoming dedication of the Salt Lake Temple during the April conference.

Mar 25 Was set apart by the First Presidency as a general fast day to all the saints of Zion to meet in their several meeting houses and ask the forgivness of each other to prepare themselves to go to the Dedication of Salt Lake Temple which was to take place on the Sixth of April and continue till the 18th holding two meetings each day, giving all claiming to be saints the privilage of attending[.] I was busy writing recommends for the Ward about 200 dividing up into 3 days part on the 7th and part on the 11th the others on the 14th. We met in our Ward nearly all attending and had a good time[.] much of the Spirit of the Lord was enjoyed in giving testimony and asking forgivness which lasted for over four hours, and at the close a vote was taken to forgive each other.

April 4 I attended the Conference in Salt Lake City with part of my family. Pres Wilford Woodruff opened by thanking the tens [of] thousands of saints for their prayers in his behalf, he said it was a day that he had looked forward to for many years of his life, namely the fininshing of the Salt Lake Temple and dedication thereof, said that a great many of the Brethren that he had labored with had gone to the spirit world[.] also thanked the Saints for their diligent efforts that they had put forth in finishing that glorious house unto the Lord and said thousand[s] would rejoice in the spirit world to know of its completion in the hope that their friends would open the prison doors to them...

April 6   The grand event commenced by the diffrent Presidents of the Varous Quorums with the general officers of the Church with a few of the Pioneer Sisters all to the number of over two thousand passed through the Temple going through the diffrent rooms which were the most beautiful places that I had ever beheld upon earth seeming to be in Heaven, the meeting was opened at 10 A.M. by Prest W. Woodruff making a few very touching remarks and the beautiful singing by the Salt Lake Choir[,] the young ladies being dressed in white, after which Prest W Woodruff offered the Dedicatory prayer which was very impressive occupying over 40 minutes, after which Prest Lorenzo Snow shouted with the people following him (swinging their Hancheifs) Hosannah, Hosannah, Hosannah to God and the Lamb, Amen, Amen, Amen, repeated three times, it was a glorious vision to behold. Presidents Woodruff, Cannon and Smith, each spoke with mighty power causing many to shed tears, a time never to be forgotten by those having that precious privilege in attendance, another company went through in the afternoon, and it was expected to take 12 or 13 days with 2 companies each day to give all claiming to be saints the privilege of going through and attending the services.

April 7 In the afternoon company I had the privilege of again going through with my wives Margaret and Emily and my son Willard R and daughters Rebecca and Lydia (others to go later on) the spirit prevailed as at the first meeting on this

171

day, an evening company went through to make up for extra ones not included in the arrainged companies.

April 8 We came home to let others go down and found all well at home, while the first services in the Temple was being held a very heavy wind storm was raging doing a great amount of damage in places, I forgot to mention that the First Presidency gave the privilage to some 500 prominent Gentiles to go through and view the inside of the Temple on the 5th before the Dedication and they were very pleased and gave a fair description of it, stating it to be the finest place they had ever beheld, it removed much prejudice from their minds toward us which had existed in the past, the news of which spread over the world....

After forty years of blood, sweat, and tears the Salt Lake Temple was complete. Perhaps now things could more or less settle into some degree of normalcy.

ON TO
STATEHOOD

Chapter Nineteen

It snowed on April 10, and no plowing had been done yet.

On April 11 Henry:

...spoke at the funeral of David Purdy who had shot himself while still weak recovering from sickness.

The last day of April was again quarterly stake conference. The brethren in attendance spoke at the first session, but some were called back to Salt Lake City as President Willford Woodruff was ill. In spite of the illness the conference was carried on the next day.

The season was late, and plowing didn't get underway until after the first of May. The end of May brought some much-needed rain; it also brought spring commencement exercises:

May 26 I attended the closing term of the B Y College[1] held in the Thatcher opera house[.] it was crowed to its utmost capacity a good program was rendered

------

[1] Brigham Young College—Logan High School is now located on the old BYC campus.

While Henry did not say, it is both likely and possible that he had children attending Brigham Young College.

Another quarterly conference had come and gone and:

> Aug 4 The case of the Logan Cow Pasture Co and John M Davidson was appealed from the Bishops court by James Quaile the Pres of the High Council, the Bishops decision was reversed after a great deal of questioning back and forth, I was requested to be present[.] they decided in favor of the Company, later it was again reversed by the Council from their first decision

On August 5, Henry reorganized the Primary association in his ward installing his daughter Rebecca as second counselor. On August 6, he was subpoenaed to Ogden to attend court in the defense of F. J. Keisel. The trial was deferred until August 9. Not wanting to waste time, Henry traveled on to Salt Lake City to attend General conference where, again, the Saints were admonished to have more home industry for themselves.

Upon returning to Ogden, Henry was involved in a rather interesting case.

> Oct 9 I returned to Ogden and attended court and gave my testimony stating that Mr Keizel only promised Cache Co $1000.00 provided they put in an Iron Bridge across Bear River at Cache Junction, but the County let the Bridge contract for $1650.00 to be built of wood and then sued Kiezel and Post his partner for the full amount they promised for the Iron, the jury decided that they should pay $500.00 and the Judge throwed the case out for a new trial or to be settled by arbitration. I returned to Cache Junction and finished putting in my crop, as we had had some fine rains, but my crop the past season had been very small only about 4[1] bushels to the acre taking it all for Bread and seed after expenses for cutting [and] thrashing but very thankful for that as some were much worse off.

---

[1] Modern farmers tend to expect crops in excess of 100 bushels per acre.

Normally such a light crop would not be worth cutting, but Henry had no choice if he wanted to feed his family.

The October quarterly conference was well attended. Several of the Apostles were present, including the two from Logan: Moses Thatcher and Marriner W. Merrill. Henry notes:

> Oct 29 ...Pres G Q Cannon said it was a great sin for the saints to send for Doctors when our families were sick instead of calling for the Elders of the Church in which we should have faith that we may be healed. The Brethren urged it upon the Saints to keep the word of Wisdom also to establish home manufactures in our midst and to stop going into debt, also said we were free with regard to our politics only not to get up ill feelings toward each other, said much of the ill feeling of the world was being removed...toward us, the church property that had been taken from us had now been returned, the Brethren all felt well in their attendance at our conference which lasted two days.

The government and the people of the Utah Territory had applied for statehood as early as 1849. Finally, after years of trying, the results of their continuing efforts were beginning to bear fruit.

> Dec 13 News came over the wires that Utah was accepted in the House by a very large majority to become a State, it now only had to wait for the Senate to give the right which was very favorable.

The year 1893 ended on a happy note.

> Dec 23 Saturday, I was very busy distributing donations to the poor for Christmans that had been brought in for that purpose, the people had been very liberal under the circumstances that [we] were in as a people.

> Dec 27 Our Ward Sunday school had a good time in a dance, and giving them [the children] candy and the Parents [candy] in the evening.

On Henry's birthday on January 27, 1894, he joined with the Primary children in a sleigh ride, and:

we had a good time

Characteristically, Henry noted the comments made in the January quarterly conference.

Jan 28 Our Stake Conference commenced, Pres Joseph F Smith and Apostles F M Lyman and M W Merrill and several of the Presidents of the Seventies were in attendance, and the house was filled to overflowing and in the afternoon an oveflow meeting was held in the East Basement. In the morning Elder Seymore B Young spoke at great length upon the faith that had been exhibited by the Prophet Joseph Smith and other early Elders of the Church in proclaiming this Gospel, and the faith that it took to establish this people in these vallies of the Mountains and the Saints needed to be very careful lest at this date, of the outside world getting an influence for evil over the youth. Elder John Morgan following upon the same subjects also advising the Brethren to stay at home and cultivate the soil and raise produce instead of importing so much and take care of our machinery[.] Elder Feildstead followed with good advice. In the afternoon Elder J G Kimball spoke for a short time upon us as people paying our tithing that we may escape the judgments of God that will be poured out upon Babylon. Pres J F Smith followed upon the same also spoke with great force upon the sins of imorallity that was creeping into the church, especially among the young, and said unless this evil was hunted out and the offender brought to justice it would bring the displeasure of our God upon us, yet we must labor with patience and kindness. At the evening meeting Apostle F M Lyman spoke at great length upon the duties of the priesthood said men should not be ordained to the higher when they had not done their duty in the lesser, and said all the Quorums should be kept busy at work. Pres. J F Smith followed upon the same strain also said when a young couple, was not worthy to go to the Temple to get married[.] the Bishop should counsel them to get married by the Bishop and let them prove themselves as worthy first.

Only two more comments were noted for the year 1894.

Feb 21 I was voted in by the City Council as Street Supervisor for the city.

Mar 1 I was qualified for the office.

Quarterly conference was convened on January 27, 1895. The Saints were again counseled to keep the Word of Wisdom and to pay their tithing, notwithstanding money was scarce and the price of grain low.

On January 30:

> I closed up my Ward tithing books the people had paid a very fair tithing[,] the most of them[,] considering the close time with every body.

Then on:

> Feb 5   I ordained my son Willard R[ussell] an Elder and William Worley ordained my son Melvin J after they had both been presented before the ward also before the priesthood meeting of the Stake as was now the order.

It is easy for us, in our day, to look back to the "good old days" and think of them as a time free of our current problems. Not so.

> Feb 6   I was subpenoed before the court held in Logan on the Mrs (name in original journal) case of man slaughter[,] she stateing that she had never received any aid from the Ward when she had continuesly for two years past and she had had a illegetimate child and it was believed she had killed it as it was found dead and buried in the lot.

Accidents once more plagued the Ballards.

> April 21   Sunday I took my wife Margaret and two of my children, Lettie and Myrtle, to Benson Ward to visit my son and Family Henry Wm, we attended Sunday School in the morning at which I spoke a few minutes, we again attended the afternoon meeting at which I again spoke, we had a good time we started home in time to get to our own Ward meeting in the evening, we got home alright, my wife got out of the buggie and the little girls remained in till I intended to take the buggie to where I had borrowed [it], but before I got fully turned around the Horse ran away and tiped the buggie over throwing me with great force to the ground upon the hard street bruising my face very badly and stunning me for over an hour that I knew nothing and was very badly shaken up, my youngest girl Myrtle was also badly bruised in the face,

Lettie was not hurt much, they carried me into the house and soon administered to me when my senses came to me, in the evening a number of the Brethern come from the meeting and again administered to me and I rested a little through the blessings of the Lord, It was through His mercies I was not hurt worse and also my children.

April 24 I sat up for a short time.

April 25 I walked out doors for a short time when the train came up from the Cache Junction my little girl Amy came up bringing the word that my son Franklin had been kicked very badly in the face with [a] horse[,] cuting his tounge and spliting his lip and knocking out one of his teeth and a few days after my little grand son Henry Wm at Benson Ward got kicked with a horse and thrown some distance but did not hurt him very bad thank the Lord.

Apostle Heber J. Grant was the only visiting General Authority from Salt Lake City for the May quarterly conference. The two Apostles from Logan were too ill to attend, and so Heber J. Grant:

...spoke nearly all the time for both days.

Among other things, he urged the practice of the Word of Wisdom, and he also said:

...our little children would grow after death to their full stature, he earnestly pleaded with the saints to keep the commandments of the Lord and He would deliver us out of our indebtedness as a people...we had a good time, we had also had a good rain for nearly a week.

June 19 We had a very severe frost which killed a great many things[,] some wheat in places.

In August sickness came calling again—an all-too-frequent and unwanted visitor.

Aug 25 My daughter Rebecca had had the Quinsy for 10 days but it broke and was a great deal better, my son H W at Benson Ward had also been sick with the same for several days and also broke which gave his ease[.] Melvin also came down with it.

Sept 15 My wife Margaret came down with it.

Winter came early to Cache Valley in 1895.

Sept 20 We had quite a snow storm[.] it snowed all the afternoon and through the night and still again in the morning till it was 8 or 9 inches deep, it broke down a great many shade trees and fruit trees, and very cold with it.

Christmas day, 1895, Henry was with his family, and they:

...spent a very agreable time together.

The year 1896 was an exciting one for all of Utah, and the excitement started right after New Year's Day. Henry notes:

Jan 4 The President of the United States signed the Bill to give unto Utah statehood[.] as it was Saturday we held a grand Holiday on the following Monday[,] in fact it was held in nearly every city and town in Utah with great rejoicing....

The goal of statehood, sought after for so many years, had finally come to pass. What a celebration[1] it must have been.

---

[1] The area for which they had originally applied for statehood would have included Utah and all, or part of, eight states surrounding Utah—it was to be called "Deseret." Although qualified to be a state according to population, the petitions were always denied.

Certain influential men suspected that Utah's pioneer leaders were disloyal and were attempting to set up their own government. It was nearly half a century before suspicion and disagreements were finally ironed out.

When the news of statehood was telegraphed to Salt Lake City, a great celebration broke loose. Guns, bells, and whistles joined in a wave of joy and happiness that swept over the State.

Little towns—unlike Salt Lake City—had no factory or train whistles, but there were plenty of tin pans, cowbells, and "six-guns." One man hung an iron pipe in front of the general store and hammered it with a steel bar, the noise echoing across the valley. Though it was winter, the weather was warm and mild. Most of the people drove to the nearby foothills where they had a community picnic around great bonfires.

Truly, this was a red-letter day in Utah's history. (Source: *Church News,* December 7, 1957.)

MARRIAGES
AND FAMILY
MISSIONARIES

Chapter Twenty

With the celebration for statehood over it was back to business as usual, and part of that business included politics. They played a small part in Henry's life, and his January 4, 1896, entry noted:

> Our City Council that had been elected last Nov now came into power and they made great changes in various officers. John Dahle was appointed in my stead as street supervisor.

Statehood apparently opened new avenues for the women that in the past had been closed to them.

> Jan 17 The Ladies of Logan had a great Banquet and Ball in the event of their first receiving their franchise in connection of Statehood for Utah, we had a good time at the Banquet[.] nearly all of Logan was out.

Two days later Apostle John W. Taylor talked in one of the Logan wards.

> ...and admonished the Saints to become one with their leaders and to acknowlege the hand of the Lord in removing the ill feeling from our outside friends...

During quarterly stake conference on February 2, the visiting General Authorities, which included Heber J. Grant, again reminded the Saints of living the Word of Wisdom and paying a generous fast offering. The Saints of Logan were asked to participate in a special fast on behalf of the Logan Apostle, Moses Thatcher, who was very ill.

Then in compliance:

Feb 6 Our Fast meeting commenced in each Ward to fast and pray for Bro Thatcher and many others that were sick in the different Wards, my daughter Rebecca was also very sick with Quinsy...

Margaret was also remembered—by another group.

April 14 Several of the Ward got together and got up a surprise upon my wife, Margaret on account of her 50th birthday[.] we had a good time together long to be remembered by all and a complete surprise to her...

The Manifesto had been presented, and a vote taken, before the congregation at the last April general conference, and:

...the first Presidency and the 12 Apostles had signed it with the exception of Bro Lund who was presiding in England,... and to the sorrow of the most of the saints Moses Thatcher had refused to sign it and thus was not sustained in his position at the conference, the other leading Elders signed it....the Manifesto was read and almost all voted for it[.] when the contrary vote was called there was only 3 or 4 voted against it, The Brethren spoke very feelingly for Bro Thatcher...

Henry was probably surprised to realize how quickly the years had passed. His and Emily's son, Willard Russell, was again baptized before marrying Bessie I. Griffin on June 10, 1896. A week later, on June 17, Melvin J. married Martha A. Jones. It was actually a double wedding as his daughter, Rebecca, married Louis S. Cardon at the same time. All three couples were married in the Logan Temple that Henry had so diligently labored to help complete. The fruits of his labors were now paying dividends.

Melvin J. had received a mission call prior to being married. A month later, on July 7, he departed for Kansas City, Missouri, leaving his bride behind.

July 24 was celebrated at Henry William's in Benson Ward. Mary Myrtle fell off a horse and pulled her arm out of its socket and:

we had to come right home with her and we got Dr O C Ormsby to put it right.

The August quarterly conference came and went with little comment, but Henry spoke of an interesting November conference.

Nov 19 Apostle Moses Thatcher was at last droped from his Quorum, he had not been sustained as an Apostle since April conference[.] he was opposed to his Quorum in matters pertaining to the Church and he failed to make it right and his priesthood was all taken from him leaving him as a member only. It was a very trying time with many on account of the way things turned out, but it was a lesson to all to take heed where we each stood....

Christmas Eve of 1896 Henry spent in Cache Junction with Emily and her children—he ended the year with a Sunday School party in Logan. Two General Authorities, Elders J. Golden Kimball and B. H. Roberts, were in attendance.

Quarterly stake conference is the subject of Henry's first entry for the year—it was January 30, 1897. The General Authorities were still concerned about the recent stand taken by one of the Apostles.

...in the morning Brigham Young Jr. spoke the most time upon obedience refering to the trouble that the Church was passing through by the opposite course that Moses Thatcher was taking against the Church and that many were taking sides with him, he proved that much kindness had been shown him.

The latter part of the conference ended on a different and interesting note.

> ...and further there was no necessity of ordaining children to the Priesthood until after they had been Baptized at 8 years[,] and where any had[,] they should be again [ordained] after they become of age.

Melvin J., though still on a mission, was greeted with an early surprise.

> Feb 5 Melvin J's wife Mattie was confined bringing him a fine son she had a very hard time[.] we had to get Dr O C Ormsby as it was before its time.

> Feb 12 I blessed it giving him the name of Melvin Russell, they were each doing well.

Just two weeks had passed when the subject of Moses Thatcher came up again—Henry was directly involved.

> Feb 14 Sunday evening we had a Sunday School review of two of the small classes and they did well, but soon after it commenced Moses Thatcher came in and the house was full in every part of it, Superintendant Joseph Quinney had charge of it and after the school was through he called upon Moses Thatcher to speak which he had no right to do without first asking me but he went on and talked for 35 minutes bringing up several grievances in the Church, said he was now thrown away like an old shoe, when he got through Bro Quinney gave out the hymn to close when I got up and demanded the privilege of speaking as Moses had brought up a great deal of his trouble in the Church with his Quorum. I spoke for a short time feeling very free as I felt it my duty to speak very plain upon his case without being excited or causing ill feeling I tried to show him wherein he should humble himself and be willing to leave his case in the hands of that noble time honored servant of God Wilford Woodruff before he should pass away. I testified in Plainess that he, Moses had been raised from his sickness by the faith and prayers and fasting of the little children together with many of their parents in the past and he should feel very humble, but afterward he wanted to speak and did try to justify himself[.] quite a number of the Brethren and sisters felt that I only did my duty.

Feb 15 I layed the matter before Pres Orson Smith and he said I did barely my duty and said I must get my counselors and Sunday School Superintendant together and find out how we stood before another Sunday to partake of the sacrament.

Feb 19   I met the above Brethren in council my first councilor N W Kimball was with me in sustaining the authorities of the Church but we had to labor very earnestly with my second councilor Lucian C Farr before he could bring his mind to it which he finnally agreed to submit to, also Superintendant Jos Quinney had to be labored with for some time before he would submit to our views which he finally did[,] his assistants felt as we did, we were together for nearly 3 hours but the time was well spent, and I felt that I had thrown a big load off my shoulders.

The Moses Thatcher business was now behind him, so Henry turned to other things.

Feb 20   John Irvines funeral was held in the meeting house[.] he was aged [and] he was a good quiet man but had withdrawn himself from the church some years ago upon very trifaling affairs but never turned against the church in any manner.

From what Henry writes, it appears that firesides have been around for a long time.

Feb 23   Pres J F Smith came up from Salt Lake City and gave a very intresting lecture before the Y.M.M.I.A. upon the origin of Mormonism showing very clearly the devine mission of Joseph Smith...

Mar 1   Mdm Mountford held four or five lectures in the Tabernacle upon village and city life in Palestine making the parables of our Saviour and His Apostlels and the Prophets very plain [—] like our every day scenes of life

A variety of things were mentioned by Henry in the next few entries: Sister Toombs died of cancer, a ward conference was held on March 28. Brother Charles O. Card was down from Canada and spoke at the conference. The various officers of the Church, stake, and ward were sustained.

Referring to the conference, Henry thought:

...the people turned out very good considering the weather which was very stormy with snow and mud upon the streets as it was a very late spring...

The last of March, Henry's grandson, Melvin Russell, was taken quite ill with "cramp colic."

...I administered to him and he got easier right away...

On April 2, 1897, Rebecca gave birth to a fine son. They named him Louis Ballard Cardon.

Quarterly conference commenced on April 17, and:

...We had very full meetings as spring had come and the roads had somewhat dried up,...

Three Apostles were in attendance, including Marriner W. Merrill, from Logan. They talked of the unity in the Quorum of the Twelve, and how a change had come over "the people as a nation." They talked about the ease the Elders had in preaching the gospel in areas previously prohibited. They advised the young to get married, and pay their tithes and offerings. They also asked for donations to help enlarge the forerunner of BYU, the Brigham Young Academy, and:

...a vote was put and carried to that effect...

The visiting Apostles were also concerned about:

...the carless habit which many of our returned missionaries got into in a short time after returning home...

Rebecca's new son was a month old on May 2, and Henry, assisted by Louis S. Cardon, the boy's father, blessed him in sacrament meeting. Melvin Russell was blessed the same day. Within a few days, however, Melvin Russell caught pneumonia. There was much illness in the area and the Ballards were concerned. Henry noted:

May 8   He was very sick at night but a little better in the morning[.] we all fasted for him during the day, Bro John H

Davis's little girls funeral was held in the Ward house on Sunday 9th.

May 15 Little Melvin Russell was very greatly improved.

Time has a way of slipping by, and on June 9, 1897, Henry and Emily's daughter, Lydia Jane, was married in the Logan Temple to William Henry Griffin. Henry and Emily were with them.

An unwelcome guest, so familiar to the Ballards, visited again before year's end.

Aug 11 Willard's wife bore him a fine daughter weighing 9 lbs.

Sept 27 She [Vivian Imogene] died after being very sick for three weeks, she suffered a great deal of pain and had been kept alive only through faith being exercised for her[.] she was a lovely sweet little darling, it was a great trial to her parents to give her up. Early in the morning Henry Wm's wife Elvira bore him a fine son and got along well. Rebecca's little boy was very sick with summer complaint.

Sept 29 Willards little girl was buried[.] there was quite a large turn out of the friends and people of Newton where it was held in the meeting house.

Henry turned sixty-six on January 27, 1898. He remembered it this way.

It was my sixty-sixth birthday and my two councilors N W Kimball and Lucian C Farr acted as a comittee and extended an invitation to all the married people of the Ward both saints and non members to attend a social gathering of the Ward in the evening at the meeting house and they nearly all turned out and all very much enjoyed themselves, and councilor Kimball presented me with a beautiful leather covered arm rocking chair which cost nearly forty dollars whereupon I made a short speech, the most of the people congratulated me upon the event of my life, the next night all the young people of the Ward over twelve years had another party, and the following day the children had a lovely time in the dance and all the Ward seemed to enjoy themselves very much for which I felt very thankful to the Lord for the respect shown to me and as I expressed myself I hoped to be still able to retain that love and affection of the Ward,

187

The following lines was composed by a freind Aaron Dewitt
which had left the church years ago[1]

To Bishop Henry Ballard, on the anniversary of his sixty-sixth Birth
day Jany 27, 1898

Another year has rolled around and added to thy age,
Thy record on the book of life has filled another page.
No line upon that register thy peace can ever mar;
Because thy life throughout, has been as stainless as a star.

We know thou art no polished gem, but natural and free;
And love the truth for its own sake, without hypocrisy.
A firm believer in the good, a helper of the race;
A comforter of every soul, of beauty and of grace.

This is the reason we are here to try our best to make;
This evening pleasant for ourselves, and for our Bishops sake.
We ask God as thy sun goes down beneath the Crimson west,
That through thy fading sight may shine the glories of the best.

That youth be given back to thee, with all its inward fire;
And kindle in thy bosom, life that never can expire.
May Heavenly mansions be revealed to thy enraptured sight;
And all thy future birthdays be as glorious as the light.

We know but few remain for thee, but as they each decay;
May friends around with living hands, strew flowers along the way.
And if the Boatman take thee first, through deaths cold flowing tide;
We will try to live that we may meet thee, on the other side.

We want thy days here, lengthened out: Thy years too, multiplied;
Until thou say it is enough, and I am satisfied.
And when thy body's laid to rest in peace beneath the sod;
May thy pure spirit take its flight back to the throne of God.

Henry's birthday party even attracted the attention of the
local newspaper. It was a memorable event for him, but life
held less surprises for the next few months. The weather,
which was always of interest to him, was mentioned several

---

[1] Aaron DeWitt and Henry had been close friends from the
time they entered Cache Valley together. Aaron chose to leave the
Church about 1868, and he became the first member of St. John's
Episcopal Church, in Logan. They were still close friends at the
time of Henry's death. (Source: *Logan Herald Journal,* February 1,
1982.)

times, and he speaks of a bad cold he had—so bad he nearly missed ward conference.

Melvin J. was still serving a succesful mission when Henry's son-in-law, Louis S. Cardon, also left for a mission in Switzerland.

Quarterly conference commenced on July 30, and the usual sage advice about payment of tithing and keeping the Word of Wisdom was disseminated, and:

> ...Also showed up the beauty of our young people selecting good companions and going to the temple...Bro Lyman promised the saints prosperity for 12 years and for them to be wise and economical and free themselves from debt...

Another son-in-law, Lydia's husband, William H. Griffin, left for a mission to England on August 19. On September 2, Church President Wilford Woodruff died in San Francisco. He was ninety-one years of age.

Decembers brought happy times for the Ballards, but this year it was special.

> Dec 9 Melvin J arrived home from his mission to the US

> Dec 11 He gave a fine discourse in the afternoon in the Tabernacle and in the evening in the Ward upon the Godhead

Henry noted on December 23, 1898, that Apostle Brigham Young, Jr., dedicated the new addition to the Brigham Young College, and Henry closed his notes for 1898 with this December 25 entry:

> Sunday was Christmas day we held meeting in the Ward in the afternoon, Melvin J gave us a fine discourse upon the birth of the Saviour and His life and labors and His Crucifiction, also of the restoration of the Gospel and the sufferings of the saints and Martrydom of the Prophet Joseph Smith and Patriach Hyrum Smith.

Henry and Margaret's son, Melvin J., was different than the average returned missionary, for on January 16, 1899, he took on the Josephites.[1]

> My son Melvin J met the Josephites according to arrangements in the Second Ward meeting house[,] he taking the stand that Brigham Young as the President of the Quorum of the twelve Apostles at the death of the prophet Joseph Smith was the authorized authority to lead the Church, he took one hour the first three nights to prove the standing to the church as it now is, while Mr Condett followed one hour for the first three [nights] to prove the stand of young Joseph. Mr Clemmonson acted as chairman, the following two nights Mr. Condett took the stand first for one [hour] each night to build up his claim while Melvin showed the folly of that stand. The sixth night it was adjourned to the Thatcher Oprea House as the second Ward hall was altogether too small to hold the people, many had to go away every night and the last Hall was too small also, Melvin was greatly blessed of the Lord in defending the true order of the Church and the saints felt well paid for following up the discussion, they came in from many of the settlements around Logan.

The first of February brought another stake conference. Apostle Lyman urged the Saints to trace their ordinations back as far as they could. Henry complied immediately.

> ...I hunted up mine and found that Apostle John Taylor had ordained me a High Priest and apostle Brigham Young ordained him on Dec 19, 1838 and the Prophet Joseph ordained him and apostles Peter[,] James and John ordained him.

Henry followed up by ordaining sixteen priests and seven deacons in the next eleven days.

Children continued to leave Henry's nest:

---

[1] Through the years, it has been a practice of the Reorganized Church of Latter Day Saints to refer to themselves as Josephites, and to the Mormon Church as the Brighamites.

Feb 22 My Daughter Lettie May was married to George Washington Squires in the Logan Temple[.] I went with my wife Margaret and son Melvin J...In the evening both families...met at my home and held a fine Wedding reception....President Isaac Smith made a fine little speech also myself and Bro John F Squires and my councilor N W Kimball.

Unpleasant things sometimes happened to the early Church members, just as they do now. Henry makes mention of another such case.

Feb 27 I held Bishops court upon the case of Fornication by [name in original journal] with [Name in original journal] we had a number of witnesses and it is proven that he had had Intercourse with her quite a few times and she was near her confinement but he refused to do anything.

(Feb) 28 we met again and give further advise and rendered our dicision which was for him to marry her or he would be cut off from the church[,] we give him two weeks to consider the matter[.] his father President [name in original journal] was satisfied with our decision and tried to reason with him and get him to marry the girl[.] we requested [name in original journal] when she got through her confinement to come before the Ward and ask their forgiveness[.] it had been a very bad case to settle and he had acted very stubern and said he would do nothing but we hoped for the best for the sake of his Parents especially his father as he wished to do right in the matter

Mar 30 I married [name in original journal] and [name in original journal] at her mothers house and his Father [name in original journal] blest their little son which was near a month old[.] he said he would not live with her

Aprl 2 Sunday afternoon [name in original journal] came before the Ward and asked forgivness of the Saints for her sin and they all forgave her except his mother and sister

Trouble, like grapes, often comes in bunches.

(Apr.) 22 Joseph Kedd cut his throat while in the Jail for stealing

(Apr.) 24 His funeral was held at his brothers house in the second Ward there was a very large turnout

(Apr.) We had quite a snow storm

191

May 4   Katie Jones daughter of Cyrus Jones funeral was held in the second Ward meeting house[.] she had been sick for a long time, she was a good young woman there was a house full of kind sympathizers

May 14   I was taken very sick[.] after going to bed I did not know anything for over half an hour.

May 24   I was a good deal better I went to the Temple with my son Ernest who was going upon a Mission[,] also my wives went with me[.]...I was called upon to speak to the saints that were going through, I felt well

June 14   My son Ernest started at 6 A. M. I went down to the Junction and visited with the family for a few days and we saw him off. He was also going with my son in law [George Washington Squires] to Calafornia on a Mission[.] they both went off cheerfully the saints were all kind to them both in Second Ward and at Newton.

As these marriages and missions were taking place, Church President Lorenzo Snow was preparing to remind the Saints of another important, somewhat neglected, principle of the Church. It is a principle he wanted reinstated and practiced.

PRESIDENT SNOW – TITHING

Chapter Twenty-One

President Lorenzo Snow, while in Saint George, had a revelation concerning the payment of tithing to help fund the debt-ridden Church. A solemn assembly was the vehicle used to announce it to the body of the Church.

Henry was invited, along with all bishops, stake presidents, and others, to attend the meeting in the Salt Lake Temple on July 2, 1899.

> July 1 I started to Salt Lake City and arrived there in the evening and had the glorious privilege of attending next day [the] 2nd[,] on fast day[,] in the Temple a Solemn Assembly of all the General Church Authorities together with the Pres of Stakes and their counselors and the Bishops of all the Wards...had been called by President Lorenzo Snow. It was the greatest event in the Church [—] there were 518 Stakes and Wards represented.

Henry must have been very impressed, for his entry concerning the meeting is long and detailed, and even includes the scriptural references made by the speakers. It will not be fully referenced here—only a few key points will be quoted.

> July 2 Every Stake in the Church was represented[.] The gates were opened at 9 A. M. and only those called were

admitted. The meeting commenced at 10, President Snow Presiding...Pres Snow then stated the object of the meeting namely the law of Tithing which had been so much neglected in the past by this people which the Lord now required them to observe but was willing to forgive the past neglect...

President Snow went on to read and comment on various sections of the Doctrine & Covenants of the Church, and then said:

...that in 12 years we had robbed the Lord of $10,000,000.00...

He returned to the D & C momentarily before pressing the notion that non-tithe payers' names should not be found on the records of the Church. This law, he said, must be adhered to before a temple recommend could be given, and:

...The Holy City will be built by the law of Consecration[,] prepare yourselves for the Redemption of Zion and the coming of the Son of Man....

President George Q. Cannon then spoke, lamenting the fact that:

...the Railroads were made in this state and owned by us and we ought to have held them...

The tithing theme was then picked up again by President Snow.

...[he] said the Lord would not forgive us any more for not paying our Tithing neither should the Bishops give any more recommends to the Temples neither would such be called to go to Jackson Co[.] the Lord will not send Hornetts this time to drive the enemy but will send siclones [cyclones] Pestilence Fire and Famine to destroy them...

Apostle George Teasdale and President Joseph F. Smith followed suit with remarks such as:

...if we pay our Tithing and offerings we comply with a law of [the] Celestial Kingdom but if we fail to do so we cannot attain to Thrones and Kingdoms...if we do not pay our Tithing we have no assurance that our enemies will not drive us from our homes...When we are judged by God it will not be by what is heard[.] there are other books kept that show [not only] what we should do but what we have done[.] we should be honest with God then we are honest with ourselves...we cannot be His children and disobey him...it is a blessing to those that pay[,] and a curse to those that disobey...Children should pay thiting when they earn anything...

In the same entry Henry noted:

...we had a good time long to be remembered[.] The meeting was dismissed a little after 7 P. M. I went to Cache Junction that night and went to Logan next day

The General Authorities of the Church left little doubt— after more than nine hours—that while the law of tithing had been in effect since biblical times, it was time to do something about it.

A month later, on August 6, stake conference was held in Logan. President Lorenzo Snow, along with other Apostles, addressed the subject again.

...the law of Tithing was spoken upon very strongly urgeing it very strongly as the mind and will of the Lord to this people and we must comply with it or the Lord would reject us but if we would do our duty from now on He would forgive us for our past neglect...

Once again the Mormons responded[1] to a call from the United States government.

Aug 21 Was a general Holiday in Logan in honor of the return of the Utah Volunteers in the Phillpine War[.] they held one in Salt Lake City on Saturday the 19th it was a grand event long to be remembered

Oct 17 I attended Hyrum Spillmans sons funeral in the second ward[.] he had died in California on his way home from the War in the Phillpines...

In spite of the distance, the body was transported from California to Logan. Henry had known the family in London

---

[1] The Mormon Battalion was used in the war against Mexico, and later Utah was asked to furnish troops for the Civil War.

while on his mission there, and they wished to have the boy's funeral in Henry's Second Ward.

It was October 29—time for stake conference again. President Snow, along with several Apostles, was in attendance. The importance of paying tithing flowed naturally from their lips, and they said paying it would:

> ...increase our faith and the things of this world...

The Brethren then spoke:

> ...upon our enemies accusing us of immoral and dishonest lives together with many other things that we were not guilty of but said we should live above these things and keep the laws of the Gospel

Lending some credibility to what "our enemies [were] accusing us of," Henry's stake president returned from an extended absence to explain to the Saints about a failed business venture that involved some of the Church members.

> ...in the afternoon Orson Smith our [Stake] Pres who had left the country six months before because he had taken wheat of many Brethren on deposit and had failed in business and not able to meet his obligations to them just returned the day before was called upon to make a statement[.] he said he was sorry for the course that he had taken and asked those that he owed to wait upon him and he would pay every cent as soon as he could and offered his resignation as Pres[.] Pres Snow spoke for some time upon the case and said he was sorry for him but thought it was the best thing to be done for his good and the good of the Stake...

The meeting was concluded with remarks from President Snow commending the Saints for their willingness to pay an increased tithing as the General Authorities had asked.

> ...Pres Snow...said that July of this year compared to last was 4 times more and Aug[,] 3 times more and Sept[,] 6 times more and Oct[,] 14 times more and yet our crops were

only about one fourth of what they were last year[.] he said the Lord would abundantly bless us for us fulfilling that law[.] he said it exceeded any other Stake in its increase...

The following day, October 30, 1899, a new stake presidency was formed.

Late fall found Henry doing the routine things: listening to lectures, going to meetings, and attending the temple for the marriage of his daughter, Jennie Lulu, who married Frank Griffin.

A December 23 entry tells of the funeral services of Robert Davidson. Robert, like Henry, had been a bishop for many years. He had suffered a great deal before he died from cancer. The funeral was held in the Logan Tabernacle.

The year ended with another funeral. This one was for the son of Apostle Marriner W. Merrill. No mention is made of the usual Christmas festivities, but he was impressed by the generosity of the members of his ward in "bringing in their offerings to the poor for Christmas."

A new century was ushered in as January 1, 1900, rolled around—it was not chronicled by Henry. Later, however, on January 16, he mentioned:

We got up an old folks party in the afternoon with dinner for all over 60 years of age in the Ward and in the evening for all married folks with a picknick and songs and dancing and speeches,...I was called [to speak] for all that had been in the church 50 years[,] there were 13 beside myself

Jan 19 ...The Logan temple and all the others were closed as the smallpox was spreading in parts of Utah

Henry's birthday, always remembered, came on January 27—he was sixty-eight. His daughter-in-law, Mattie:

...got up a family sociable with a number of friends...

Quarterly stake conference convened on January 28, and the theme from the Brethren was, again, the payment of tithing and keeping out of debt. Also mentioned was:

> ...[to] not follow after the fashion's of the world as we had been called out of the World to build up the Kingdom of God upon the earth...

On February 2, Henry was seriously injured when he was thrown off his wagon and landed on his head:

> ...which very much hurt it and the cords of my neck as I could do nothing for some time[,] and a week afterwards I took a very bad Dizzy spell for an hour

A month later a prayer circle, consisting of the high priests of the stake, was organized to administer to Henry.

Henry felt well enough to attend priesthood meeting on March 3, where President Joseph F. Smith was to speak. He spoke of:

> ...the carelessness of many parents in not teaching their children to principles of the Gospel...

The campaign for more tithing money was still going on—Apostle Merrill said:

> ...he was surprised to find so many non Tithe payers in the Stake although the Tithing had increased very much over the year before[.] there were 18 non tithe payers in our Ward still there was about $400.00 more paid this year.

In spite of the huge increase in the payment of tithes there were other financial needs that tithing money did not provide for.

> Mar 16 A special Priesthood meeting was called to consider the debts of the Stake[,] namely the B Y Monument and B Y College Building[,] also the debt upon the Logan Tabernacle which the Bishops all agreed to collect as soon as they could

The balance of the March entries are routine: ward conference, the funeral of Emma Jenks, and on April 12, Melvin J.'s son Russell fell and broke his arm.

Margaret's birthday was April 14—two days later a small party was held for her at her home in Logan.

Tithing would be mentioned again, even though the Saints had responded very generously. Henry and other bishops did all they could to further full tithe payment. Readers may recall Henry's previous entries referring to how faithfully the Saints, "the most of them," had paid tithing "considering the close time with every body," or the times when they "came up short."

The years had taken their toll on Henry. Life had been wonderful—and not so wonderful—at the same time. The combined debilitating effects of his old complaints "the gravel," the numerous sore throats, the accidents, the trials of grasshoppers, Indians, and federal agents through the years had made it more difficult for Henry to do all the things he wanted to do.

Maybe it was time for a change.

PATRIARCH
HENRY BALLARD

Chapter Twenty-Two

It is reasonable to assume that Henry had given a great deal of thought, in advance, to what he was about to do; no one can tell it better than Henry.

April 22 I sent in my resignation as Bishop of the Ward on account of failing health[,] which position I had occupied 39 years 8 days

April 26 Apostle F M Lyman and the Presidency of the Stake called a meeting of the Priesthood of the Ward in the meeting house and presented my resignation and I was honorably released by all the Brethren and they were well satisfied with my labors and a ballot was passed [as to] who should be the Bishop of the Ward and it fell upon Anton Anderson [my] former 2nd councilor[,] and Bro Lyman said it was the choice of the Presidency of the Stake as well as himself and he asked me if he was a worthy man for Bishop[.] I said he was my choice and he got a full vote of the House. Bro Lyman gave us some good council on our duties and appointed a general meeting of all the Ward to be held at 10 A. M. the following morning.

April 27 The General meeting of the Ward commenced at 10 A. M. Apostles Merrill and Lyman and the Presidency of the stake were in attendance and Anton Anderson's choice of Councilors was William Worley and Melvin J Ballard and they were each one set apart to their several offices. Bro Lyman ordained my son a High Priest and ordained him a counselor[.] my release was presented before the people the Brethren stating their satisfaction of my long labors in the Bishopric and I was honorably released and fully sustained by the saints and Apostle Lyman said they intended to ordain me a patriarch, they each gave us words of council stating that Pres Lorenzo Snow wished the people labored with to stir up the slothful ones more to their duties and encourage those who had been faithful to be more energetic for the Lord would cut His work short, but if the non tithe payers would wake up to their duties the Lord would forgive the past, but they themselves would suffer the loss to what blessings they might have enjoyed[.] there was a good spirit and feeling in the meeting[,] many cried when I was released[.] it would be a time long to be remembered by me and my family also of the Ward

Two days later on, April 29, 1900, quarterly stake conference started. Three Apostles were in attendance, including Apostle Merrill of Logan. The theme was, as had been for some time, the payment of tithing. The bishops were asked to:

...stir up the people to their duties hoping there would be less non tithe payers at the close of the year...He presented George W Ferrell and Henry Hughs who had been released as being Bishops to be ordained Patriarchs and to travel and give Blessings[.] he also presented me to be ordained one but not expected to travel unless the Lord improved my health, we were each sustained with a full vote to be ordained the following day after being presented before the conference...

April 30 Apostle Lyman...presented the above Brethren and myself as Patriarchs in the church, at the close of the forenoon meeting we were each one ordained, Apostle M W Merrill ordained me, giving me a good Blessing said if I would seek the Lord my tounge should become as a ready writer and should enjoy the spirit of that calling[.] Wilford Woodruff ordained him and Brigham Young ordained him and he was ordained under the hands of Oliver Cowdery and he was ordained by Peter, James and John...Brother Lyman then spoke to us very plainly upon our various duties said we should all keep the word of wisdom[.] he asked me if I kept the word of wisdom[,] I told him Yes I had been trying to for a great many years[,] he then put the question to see how many had not kept it[,] 3 or 4 said they had not kept it he said they must now keep it from now on or they should have but little influence[.] he said the Patriarchs must have their Blessings well written and recorded and not to seek to give some wonderful Blessing more that what the spirit of the Lord would manifest in plainess and calmness and that spirit would prompt what to say and not to make a charge[1] but whatever the saints could aford to give to pay expencess it was alright...

Decoration Day, May 30, 1900, found Henry at the gravesites of his parents and deceased children.

Then on:

June 19 The Bishopric of the Ward got up a very pleasant sociable for the retiring Bishopric[,] there were about 300 of the Ward in attendance and [we had] a very agreable time[.] there were a great many exercises and they made me a present of a fine silk gold mounted umbrella costing about $15.00...it was a time long to be remembered

Though no longer a bishop, Henry still participated in many funerals and was called upon to speak on a regular basis—often at the request of the deceased prior to their death.

Wm Nelson who used to live in this Ward died and his funeral was held in the meeting house[.] I was called upon to speak[.] there was a mixed congregation of non saints

C J Larsen's first wife's funeral was held in the Tabernacle[.] I was called upon to speak as it was her request

The funeral of Cyrus W Card was held in the Tabernacle I was called upon to speak first

---

[1] No charge was made for a blessing, but a small fee could be made to cover the cost of having the blessing recorded in shorthand and then written, or typed, for the recipient.

Henry noted the events of the quarterly stake conference that commenced on July 29; he also noted the same day:

> My wife Emily brought my daughter Amy up sick from the Junction late at night we got a Doctor and he thought it was pentocietus [appendicitis] we administered to her she was very sick

> July 30 We got Apostles Clawson and Smoot to come down to my house and administer to her[.] we administered to her several times ourselves

> Aug 3 Amy commenced to get a little better but she had been very sick[.] we administered to her very often and tried to exercise all the faith we could for her

> Aug 25 Amy and her mother returned to the Junction[.] She was now much improved through the Blessings of the Lord

William H. Griffin, Henry's son-in-law, returned home from his mission in England. He had:

> ...visited my Nephew George Ballard and family in London they treated him very kind

It appears, however, William had no more success converting his relatives in England than Henry, and probably felt a little like Henry did when Henry was prompted to write in London on March 15, 1887:

> I returned back to the office feeling that I had but very few friends among my relatives

The last entry Henry made in the year 1900 concerned the death of another family member.

> Dec 6 My Mother in Law Janet McNeil died after being sick for 2 years[,] she bore it very patiently during that length of time[.] she requested her son James R and my son Melvin J to speak at her funeral which they did. It was held the following Sunday on the 9th in the Logan Tabernacle[.] It was a very large congregation she was a very faithful Latter Day Saint of about 50 years. She left now living[,] 6 living children 37 grandchildren and 19 great grandchildren for whom she set a good example for them to follow

An epidemic of smallpox ushered in the new year, 1901. Willard R.'s wife contracted and recovered from the disease.

Most of Henry's entries, until the next quarterly stake conference, concerned the funerals of his contemporaries. As in the past, Henry was often asked to speak on such occasions.

Among those contemporaries was President George Q. Cannon who died in California where he had gone for his health. President Cannon was seventy-five years old at the time of his death.

Until 1901 nearly all, if not all, of Cache Valley consisted of but one stake—the Cache Stake—but on:

April 28 Our conference was held [and] we had a very large turn out[.] the Stake was divided into three[,] ours was the center still called the Cache [Stake][,]...and the North part of the Stake was named Benson Stake[1]...and the South part was named Hyrum Stake...it was a time long to be remembered

About three weeks later, Henry penned this note:

May 5 Sunday was forty years since I was married to Margaret and we got part of the family and a few of our friends together and enjoyed ourselves and our sons and daughters presented their mother with a gold watch and myself a Gold ring which was very kind of them. Sister Lucy L Cook presented us with the following poetry.

To Brother and sister Ballard on their Fortieth Wedding Day

Hail Patriarch Father, honored mother
We meet you this auispicious day,
And with heartfelt kindly greetings,
For your happiness we pray.

We celebrate the anniversary
Of your Fortieth Wedding Day

---

[1] Named after Ezra T. Benson, not Benson Ward, which was also named to honor him.

In each others love rejoicing,
God had been with you all the way

Long ago a man and maiden,
With no gaudy outward show,
Heart and hand by Heaven united
Started out through life to go.

But a child in years the maiden,
Still a woman's heart was there,
And the man was brave and noble,
Well might she trust to his fond care.

They had naught, the world called riches,
But their hopes, their lives were one,
Rich in faith they lived the Gospel,
Of the Lord and His dear Son.

Trials they meet and sacrifices,
Hardships, toils and many cares;
But they have been true and faithful,
Still life to them is very fair.

Age comes on with silver tresses
But the Heavens peace is with them still,
Patiently they yet are struggling
To serve, and do the Father's will.

They now are rich, priceless jewels
In their crown of life they wear
Bright immortal souls were given them
Which they've reared and trained with care.

No dark sorrow in their bosoms
For a jewel lost through sin
They have bravely fought life's battle
And the victory they'll win.

Brother Ballard, Sister Ballard
Take your friends best wishes now
May your happiness continue
May the years with garlands deck your brow.

Time passed quickly. Henry's son, Ernest Russell, was home from his mission by late May. A few days later

Henry's son-in-law, George W. Squires, returned from his mission. Both had served in California.

Weather, often noted by Henry, is mentioned again:

> May 23 We had a very heavy wind storm that blew down hundreds of trees in Logan and 10 barns and a great deal of damage also in numerous of the other settlements doing the same.

Amy, Henry and Emily's daughter who had been ill earlier, was thought to be healed; apparently she was not.

> July 2 My wife Emily brought my daughter Amy up sick from the Junction with Pentocietus [appendicitis] she was very sick
>
> (July 5) Dr Parkinson and Dr Budge performed an opperation upon her she took it very good

Later in July during quarterly stake conference, Henry was asked to bear his testimony after which Apostle Marriner W. Merrill noted that he and Henry had came into the Church about the same time—fifty-two years ago.

Henry's journal lay silent until October 10, 1901. He then noted:

> President Lorenzo Snow died in Salt Lake City he was at the conference at one meeting on the 6th and spoke[.] his funeral was held on Sunday and his body was brought to Brigham City to be burried where he had lived so long...

A few days later Henry's thoughts turned again to Amy.

> Oct 15 My daughter Amy died at Cache Junction after being sick so long[.] we had exercised all the faith we could for her, but it seemed like it was the will of the Lord for her to pass from us although it was a hard trial for us especially for her mother as she was the youngest
>
> Oct 17 The funeral was held at Newton all the family was in attendance and many of the saints of that settlement[.] there was a very kind feeling she was loved by all who knew her and she had filled her mission on earth

The same day as Amy's funeral the First Presidency of the Church was reorganized. Uncharacteristically, Henry made a separate entry dated that same day.

> Oct 17 The First Presidency was reorganized Joseph F Smith was chosen and set apart as President and John R Winder as first and Anthon H Lund as second councilors was each sustained by the Quorum of Apostles and a general confrence was called to be held on the 10th of Nov to sustain the selection of the Twelve Apostles

During the balance of the year Henry mentions only the stake conference and ends the year 1901 with this special note:

> Dec 27 A dinner and entertainment was gotten up in our Ward by the Relief Society for the Old Folks over 60 years of age[.] there was a good social time with all[.] several were called upon for a song and some for a speech[.] I was called for one which I gave

Although not mentioned, poor health must have been a problem for Henry. Nothing else could have kept him from his regular visits to his journal. From this point on, there are few entries, and nearly all of them are printed here without comment.

> Jan 8, 1902 My son Franklin went to the Temple and was married to Sarah Stevens of Newton

> April 21 We had quite a snow storm

> Aug 12 We had a good time on the [Tabernacle] square of the old folks over 60[.] I was called upon as Chaplin

> Sept 10 My daughter Lydia went to the Temple and got Endowments for my daughter Amy who died and she [Amy] was sealed to Ezra Cardon[1] a son of Paul who had died some time ago

---

[1] Amy came to Emily in a dream with Ezra Cardon by her side. He had died shortly after Amy passed away. This dream came to Emily three different times, and Ezra was always with her. A

May 7, 1903 My wife Emily died after being sick for a long time at Cache Junction

May 10 The funeral was held at Newton there was a very large meeting and 32 teams followed her[.] there was a very kind feeling at the meeting with good teaching[,] and exhortation showing great respect to the family

Jan 27, 1904 Was my 72nd birthday we had all of my family together in Logan[.] there were 11 children and my wife Margaret and 22 grandchildren 4 son in laws and 5 daughter in laws We had a good time of socialability

Jan 29 We had an old folks entertainment in the Ward I was called to ask a blessing and to give a speech we had a good time altogether

June 22 Ernest Reid Ballard was married in the Logan Temple to Amandia [Amanda] Miller of Newton

Nov 24 We had an old folks entertainment in the Ward we had a good time I was called to ask a blessing and to give a speech which I enjoyed

Henry's journal entries ended abruptly and appropriately, with a good time, a blessing, and a speech. Henry himself continued on for a few more years.

Little is written of Henry's activities during his remaining four years, except in retrospect. One event did occur, however, not of Henry's making, but rather by way of tribute to a worthy pioneer.

A large portrait of Henry had been prepared for display in the Logan Second Ward where he labored as bishop for 39 years and eight days. The unveiling was set for his 74th birthday, January 27, 1906, and a beautiful program was prepared to accompany the unveiling of the painting.

---

similar manifestation came to Ezra's father. Emily and Brother Cardon felt impressed that it was the desire of these young people to be sealed to each other as man and wife for eternity.

A sketch of Henry's life was read, and his son, Melvin J., noted for his beautiful voice, sang. Tributes were paid, and poetry was written and recited to celebrate the occasion. Commenting on the event the *Logan Journal* said:

> Seldom has a citizen of Logan been paid a finer tribute than the one bestowed upon Bishop Ballard yesterday.

As was often the case, Henry was called upon to speak, and in part of his speech he said:

> It is a great pleasure to me to meet with you and see so many familiar faces that have fought the fight of life with me.
>
> It is fifty-seven years next month since I embraced the truth, and how thankful I am that I have kept the faith, and still have an abiding testimony concerning it. I have passed through many hardships but in them all I have witnessed the hand of the Lord and kept the faith. It is the faithful, everyday life that we lead that counts in the end and meets the demands of justice. I am grateful for the kindly feeling manifested toward me here today. I am grateful for my family, and hope whatever may come in their pathway, they will prove true to the faith, and be worthy of eternal life.
>
> Brethren and Sisters, do not stumble on the faults of others, and fall by the wayside, keep straight on, in the path of truth and duty, even if you have to sacrifice your lives as others have done, for the Gospel, and great will be your reward.
>
> May the Lord ever bless you and help you through life, is my prayer for you all, in the name of Jesus, Amen.

Nothing more is mentioned about Henry until his death on February 26, 1908, at his home, in his beloved Logan.

Henry's passing was chronicled in several leading news papers including the *Deseret News*. The tributes paid to his memory are legendary. A Logan paper had this to say:

> Patriarch Henry Ballard, of the Second ward, died at his home Wednesday night at 11 o'clock, the result of general debility due to old age and cessation from a very active life. For about five years the gentleman had awaited the final summons, and it came to him peacefully. He was

unconscious some time before his death but in the last moments aroused himself, recognized the relatives about him and passed away gently.

In this passing a man widely known for his genuine worth has gone. Bishop Ballard was unassuming and one of the kind of men who would prefer to be wronged than to do a wrong. He was a very energetic man while in good health and was identified with most of the progress of the valley. He was kindly and considerate with a heart full of love for every man, and throughout his life enjoyed the respect and esteem of his fellows.

The following tribute to Henry was penned by his daughter, Myrtle Ballard Shurtliff.

He was not a hero, as we estimate men nowadays, just a plain, honest man, one of the noblest, grandest characters the writer ever knew, at once an inspiration and an ideal. He was one of those magnificent men who had the rare courage to suffer in silence for the right and never wince, being content to do the right as he saw it, without reward other than the approval of his own conscience and without fear of the consequences. If honesty, love of human kind, loyalty, courage and consistency count for aught in the Master's realm, then Henry Ballard will have abounding wealth in the regions beyond.

May his sleep be as peaceful as his life was worthy, and his memory live to strengthen and inspire those he reluctantly left.

It was a leap year when Henry was quietly laid to rest in the Logan cemetery on Sunday, March 1, 1908. His wife Margaret now rests beside him, and they are surrounded by many of their loved ones—just the way Henry would have wanted it.

Whatever tributes and eulogies were made in Henry's behalf, and they were legion in number, were well deserved. They might have even fallen a little short—it is difficult to find the words necessary to describe such a gentle giant of a man.

Henry Ballard was one of the most revered men ever to grace Cache Valley with his presence. His journal is widely quoted, even to this day, and it is considered to be one of the best histories available of his time.

Henry's time was "a time long to be remembered." Certainly Henry's passing "put a quietus upon" the people of Cache Valley.

May the legacy of Henry Ballard never die.

Ever.

MARGARET'S
AUTOBIOGRAPHY

My birthplace, Tranent, was a small village located near the sea shore on the banks of the mouth of the Firth of Forth not many miles from Edinburgh. From the village one may view the beautiful scenes of grasses and hills and waters so typical of picturesque Scotland.

When I was five years old my little baby brother Peter Reid McNeil died. He was only one year old. His death made me very sad and I cried over it many times. He was buried in the church yard at Tranent

When I was eight years old my father baptized me a member of the Church of Jesus Christ of Latter-day Saints—it was May 28, 1854. He had joined the Church and was baptized when I was about a year old. He was a coal miner and had to be at work every morning at four o'clock. Therefore, when I was baptized, I had to go early in the morning. It was a beautiful May morning when I walked to the sea shore. We carried a lantern to light our way. As I came up out of the water, the day was just beginning to dawn, and the light was beginning to creep over the eastern hills. It was a very beautiful sight—one that I shall never forget. At this time I was filled with a sweet heavenly spirit which has remained with me to this day.

That night all of the saints met at our home and I was confirmed a member of the Church of Jesus Christ of Latter-day Saints. I was given my choice to either sing, pray or bear my testimony. I offered up a simple prayer, for my heart was filled with great joy and thanks to God for the privilege of becoming a member of His Church, and this gratitude has remained in my heart and has increased as the years have gone by.

The first ten years of my childhood was spent in Tranent, but because of being a "Mormon" I was not permitted to attend the schools, and so I was entirely deprived of schooling while in the old country, and in pioneering there was little opportunity for education. During those ten years our family enjoyed the association of the Elders and Saints. My father was President of the Edinburgh Conference for a number of years. Therefore, the Elders visited our home often, and we were always glad to receive them, although many times I went to bed hungry in order to give my meal to the visiting Elders.

We had waited a long time to come to Zion, but my father was called by the Church to stay in Scotland and preside over the Saints in that Branch. When Father was finally given the chance to leave Scotland he tried to persuade my mother to wait awhile—Mother was about to give birth to her sixth child. Mother insisted upon coming for she had faith that the Lord would take care of her.

Before we left, my mother took us to say good-bye to our grandmother, my mother's mother, Margaret (Martin) Reid, but she would not come to the door or let us in. My aunt came to the door and said Grandmother didn't want to see us for we had broken her heart because we had joined the Mormon Church. Mother took us by the hand and we went home. Mother cried all the way home.

On April 27, 1856 we left Liverpool for America. There was a large company leaving. My mother was not well and was taken on board ship before the time of sailing while the sailors were still disinfecting and renovating the ship. Here my brother Charles was born with only one woman on board the ship to attend my mother. When the Captain and doctor came on board the ship and found that a baby had been born, they were delighted and thought it would bring good luck to the company. They asked for the privilege of naming him. Brother Willie, President of the company, thought it best to let the Captain name him as there were eight hundred passengers and nearly all of them were "Mormons." He was named Charles Collins Thornton McNeil—Charles Collins after the Captain and Thornton after the boat .

We were on the ocean for nearly six weeks, and at the end of this long tiresome journey, we landed at Castle Gardens, New York.

During this time we had many hardships to endure, but through it all we were greatly blessed. Because of my mother's condition, and my being the oldest member of the family and being blessed with health, I had to share the responsibility with my father of taking care of the rest of the family who suffered greatly with sea sickness. On board ship we had to prepare our own food and were permitted to take our turn using a stove which was provided for the company. I was the cook for the family and sometimes experienced trouble in preparing our porridge which was about all we had to eat. I was but ten years old and somewhat of a venturesome spirit, and through this perhaps met many more difficulties than I would have done otherwise. However I was protected from accident and blessed with health the entire trip.

After landing we planned to go west to Utah with the handcart company, but President Franklin D. Richards counseled my father not to go in that company. Afterwards, we were very thankful because of the great suffering, privation, and cold weather to which these people were subjected. There were many of the company who were frozen that year on their journey.

My father was then advised to go to St. Louis, spend the winter there and then prepare to go through to Utah the next year. While we were in St. Louis my little brother John Reid died. He was three and one half years old and was buried there. During the winter my father worked and saved his money, but when spring came he was called on a mission to help make a new settlement 100 miles west of civilization. It would be called Genoa, and was to be a temporary settlement for the benefit of the immigrating Saints.

We left St. Louis on the steam boat and came up the Missouri River. The measles broke out while we were on the boat and all of my mother's children except me took them and were very sick. When we landed we camped on the bank of the river until our teams and wagons came.

When we were all ready to start on our journey westward, my father's team of five-year old unbroken oxen ran away, and we were delayed. We had never seen oxen before, and the animals allotted to us had to be roped and tied in order to yoke and fasten them to the wagon. When they were released from the ropes they became unmanageable and difficult to catch.

The company had gone on ahead, and as my mother was anxious for me to go with them she strapped my little brother, James, on my back with a shawl. He was only four years old and still quite sick with the measles, but I took him since mother had all she could do to care for the other children. I hurried and caught up with the company traveling with them all day. That night a kind lady helped me take my brother off my back. I sat up and held him on my lap with the shawl wrapped around him, alone, all night. He was a little better in the morning. The people in the camp were very good to us and gave us a little fried bacon and some bread for breakfast.

We traveled this way for about a week, my brother and I not seeing our mother during this time. Each morning one of the men would write a note and put it in the slit of a willow stuck into the ground to tell how we were getting along. In this way mother knew that we were all right.

We crossed the Elkhorn River. The ferry took the wagons across, but the animals had to swim.

I arrived in the place which was called Genoa ahead of the company, thus becoming the first female resident of the present city of Genoa.[1]

We stayed in Genoa about two years during which time we had very little to eat as the people were all very poor. We raised corn but the frost came early and it did not ripen well. We had to dry it in the oven and it was so nearly spoiled that we had to open the door while it was drying because the smell was so offensive, but it was all we had to eat. We had only one hand grinder for the whole company to use which belonged to Brother Sleight. Of course it kept us very busy grinding. During the settlement of Genoa we also suffered

---

[1] The following was taken from the Church history of Genoa. "In passing it may here be stated that sister Margaret McNeil, a girl of twelve years of age, arrived on the present site of Genoa ahead of the main company in 1857, and was the first female in camp. The company consisted of ninety-seven men, twenty-five women, forty children, forty-two yoke of oxen, twenty cows, six horses, twenty-four chickens, twenty hogs, two cats, and dogs a plenty."

much from hostile Indians. They were very troublesome, and we were always in danger.

After we had made this settlement my father was called to another place called Woodriver. It was about one hundred miles west of Genoa which made it about two hundred miles from civilization. This was a very pretty place surrounded by elm trees. While at Genoa my brother, Joseph McNeil was born on January 14, 1859, so when we left for Woodriver, Mother had a very young baby to care for making travel difficult.

When we left Genoa, we had to cross the Loup Fork River. A ferry was built for the wagons, but the animals had to swim across. We traveled down the north side of the Platte River and reached the new settlement. Woodriver was a general stopping place on the immigrant route through the Platte Valley.

One day while we were at Woodriver, our cow ran away from us, and when father found that she was lost, he sent my brother Thomas and me to hunt for her. We looked all day but were unable to find her. Starting out early the next morning we continued the hunt and looked all that day. Toward evening we were going down along the Platte River, and as we looked down the river we saw three large Sioux Indians coming towards us on horses. They seemed very war-like, and I was afraid they were going to carry us away with them. So I said to my brother, "Let us pray". We were running as fast as we could and still praying all the time although we were unable to get down on our knees.

The Indians soon came right up to us and wanted us to go with them. We were trying to be brave and told them we were on our way home and pointed toward our house for we could see the smoke coming out of our chimney. One of the Indians tried to pull my brother up on his horse, but Thomas was heavier than the Indian expected and slipped from his grasp and dodged right under the horse's belly, between fore and hind legs, and we ran until overtaken again. The Indians laughed and had a good time at our efforts to elude them, but in our maneuvers we were getting nearer home. I asked them to go home with us and promised that my mother would give them coffee and biscuits. I was shaking all over with fright and could hardly speak, but pointed to where the men were working. The Indians left us and went over to the men who were working. Then later they came to our house and mother gave them a nice warm supper, and they went away peaceable. Our Heavenly Father surely blessed and protected us on this occasion, for which we were very grateful.

We did not stay at Woodriver very long because the Indians were so troublesome. My father began to make preparations to go on to Utah, and when the next company came, we were ready. Woodriver was abandoned along with the splendid growing crops. The Captain of the company was pleased to have us travel with him and was very kind to us.

We had to cross the Platte River in which there were so many sand bars that it made crossing very dangerous. The men were helping the women over, but my mother was so anxious to get started that she waded in with a baby in her arms, thinking she could go through alone. She had gone but a little way when she began sinking into the quicksand and was going down very fast. Some of the men saw her and ran to her assistance. It was a difficult task to get her out and we felt that she had a very narrow escape. We had many such experiences while crossing the rivers.

One night our cow ran away from camp and I was sent out to bring her back. I was barefooted and not watching where I was going. All of sudden I began to feel that I was walking on something soft and looked down to see what it could be. I found to my horror that I was standing in a bed of snakes, large ones and small ones. At the sight of them I became so weak that I could scarcely move. All I could think of was to pray. The Lord blessed and watched out for me so that I was protected from many similar experiences.

While crossing the plains my mother's health was very poor so I tried to assist her as much as I could. Every morning I would get up early and get breakfast for the family and milk the cow so that I could hurry and drive her ahead of the company and let her eat in the grassy places until they passed on ahead, and then I would hurry and catch up with them. The cow furnished us our chief source of food, and it was, therefore, important to see that she was fed as well as circumstances allowed. In this way, the cow gave plenty of good rich milk, and we felt that had it not been for her we would have surely starved.

Being alone much of the time I had to get across the rivers as best as I could. Our cow was a Jersey and had a long tail. When it became necessary to cross the rivers I would wind the end of her tail around my hand and swim across with her.

I was always very careful to watch for every bit of wood I could find on the way. Our fuel consisted mostly of "buffalo chips," and each morning I would gather a large apron full of them for the camp fires on which we cooked our meals. At the end of each day's journey I milked my cow and helped prepare our supper after which I gladly fell asleep wherever my bed happened to be.

We traveled very slowly until we reached "Sweet Water." Here there was a terrible storm. The Captain got on his horse and scouted around to see if he could find a place of safety. It was snowing and the wind was blowing a terrific gale and we despaired for our lives. The Captain found shelter down at the bottom of a hollow. We camped here for several days until the storm abated. I was very brave and wanted to go out and explore this new camping ground. I had not gone far when I saw a large ox grazing a little way from where camp was. I ran and told my father and he and some of the men went out and killed it for the company. The discovery of this ox, I thought, was wonderful, and I felt it very providential, as we were almost starving.

In leaving this camp we had not gone far when we met Patriarch John Smith and Brother John P. Green who were going on missions and were traveling with a mule team. Father went to them for advice and told them of our circumstances. Brother Smith blessed my father and gave him ten dollars, and Brother Green gave him five dollars. Brother Smith told father to leave the Company and go on as fast as possible for it was getting cold and we were short of food. He told us to go through Weber Canyon into Ogden as it was much quicker. With the money that was given him, father bought fifty pounds of flour, it being $20.00 a hundred at Fort Laramie. We also got a little meat. Brother Smith advised my father to stay in Ogden until he earned enough food to put us through the winter, and then to go on to Cache Valley and take up land there.

We started on our journey alone and had a very hard time of it. Our food gave out and we had nothing but milk and wild rose berries to eat. However we did have a good team and could travel fast. We arrived in Ogden on the 4th day of October, 1859 after a journey of 1,035 miles from Woodriver. Although each day was filled with hardship and hunger, we thanked our Heavenly Father for His protecting care—care that made our trip easier to endure. I walked every step of the way across the plains, drove my cow and a large part of the way carried my little brother, James, on my back.

We camped on the outskirts of town, and father left us and went on into Ogden to find work. While camping here many people passed us on their way to attend the General Conference of the Church held in Salt Lake City.

Across the field from where we were was a little home and out in the yard was a big pile of squash. We were so famished that my mother sent me over to beg for squash, for we did not have a cent of money, and some of the children were very weak for want of food. I knocked at the door and an old lady came and said, "Come in, come in. I knew you were coming and have been told to give you food." She gave me a large loaf of fresh bread and said to tell my mother that she would come over soon. It was not long until she did come and brought us a nicely cooked dinner, something we had not had for a long time. This woman was surely inspired of the Lord to help us and we were grateful for her kindness. Bread never tasted so good before or since.

When father came back to us, he had found a man whom he had known in Scotland. This man took us into his home, and we stayed there until we were ready to go to Cache Valley. We all worked. Mother took the smaller children and husked corn. I herded cattle, and father and my brother worked on the threshing machine. When we had a sufficient supply of food we left Ogden and had not gone far when we met Henry Ballard and Aaron DeWitt who had been to conference, and were returning to their homes in Cache Valley. This was my first meeting with my husband. At the time of this meeting I was a barefooted, sun-burned little girl, driving my cow along the dusty country road, but it was impressed on my mother and to my husband at that time that I would some day be his wife. Brother Ballard and Aaron DeWitt helped us greatly during our journey as we traveled together to Cache Valley. When we got to the Logan River the water was so high that it lifted the box right off the wheels and we had some difficulty in getting across. We arrived in Logan October 21, 1859.

We camped in a fort made for protection from the Indians. We were in the last fort which extended from the corner of Main and Center Streets to what is known as 3rd West Street now. My father worked to get enough hay for the cattle and then went to the canyon and hauled logs to make a house. We had no lumber nor glass, so for the doors and windows we wove willows together and plastered them with clay. We used bulrushes and willows for the roof and carpet. We were very comfortable until spring. My father and brother worked in the canyon all winter gathering logs which they exchanged for bran or bacon or anything else we could eat.

At one time we ran right out of everything to eat and father had a few logs he could spare, so he went to a man and asked him if he would not give him some bran for them. This is all we had to eat for some time. This man found that we were in dire need of help and told the Presiding Elder that we needed assistance. A meeting was held and the people were told that they should pay fast offerings, which they did. The first fast offerings paid in Logan were then given to my father.

Father soon got work building a bridge, and after this we did not have it so hard. I carried water for the family all that winter from the north branch of Logan River which was about three blocks away. I had very little clothing on my body, and my feet were bare, often leaving blood stains on the snow. Sometimes I would wrap them in old rags but this was worse than ever because the rags froze to my feet.

We stayed in the fort until spring. Then we moved to a lot on Fifth West between Third and Fourth South streets. My parents lived on this lot the rest of their lives. Father built a two room adobe house, later adding three more rooms to it. I helped make the brick by tromping straw into the clay.

Early in the spring I went to work for Thomas E. Ricks for one dollar a week. I was working to get seed wheat for us to plant. The wheat was $5.00 a bushel. Brother Ricks needed a man to plow and asked father if he could spare one of his boys. Father said he would let him know that night. When I got home, he asked me if I would help him plow so my brother could work for Mr. Ricks. He would be paid two dollars a week, and this would help pay for the seed wheat much more quickly.

While my brother went to work for Mr. Ricks, I drove the cattle while father held the plow. Thus we broke the ground for the first crops that we planted in Logan. After the ploughing was finished, I went back to Brother Ricks and worked there until fall. I returned home to glean wheat, so that we would have enough bread for winter, and then went back to the Ricks' home where I worked all winter.

Next spring Grandma Thatcher offered me $1.25 a week, and as the work was easier, I went to her place and worked all summer. It was at the Thatcher home that I learned refinement and culture. I was fresh from the plains and wild as a "March Hare." It was part of my work to wait on tables, and I was so frightened I said I couldn't do it, but Grandma Thatcher would say. "Yes you can, go in there, and act like a lady." With her patience and instruction I became more confident and naturally absorbed lady-like manners that have stayed with me throughout my life.

The first grist mill was being built in Logan, and since the builders were living with Thatchers, she needed me during this time. In the fall the workman left, and her sons went to Salt Lake to school so I went again to work for Mrs. Ricks and stayed there until spring.

In January Brother Ballard asked me to go to a dance with him at Providence, a little village several miles from Logan. We had a yoke of oxen and a heavy sleigh. It was very cold and snowed a three foot wall while we were at the dance. We were unable to come home so we sat up all the rest of the night for there was not room for so many of us to go to bed in one little log house. We had a very hard time in getting home the next day. So you see, even courting had its hardships in the Pioneer days.

I had been keeping company with Brother Ballard for some time, and although I was but fifteen years old, he wanted to marry me. He felt that he could take care of and provide for me without my having to work as hard as I had been doing. We were married on Sunday, May 5, 1861, by Bishop William B. Preston. I was fifteen and Henry was twenty-nine years old. He had been put in as Bishop of Logan Second Ward a month before our marriage. Thus at the age of fifteen I became a Bishop's wife.

The following summer we had a great deal of trouble with the Indians. They were very hostile, and often the people had to seek shelter in a large cellar. I have seen the Indians ride on their horses into the yard and tramp the gardens to pieces and even go into the houses on horse back. They did an enormous amount of damage in the fields. This was the worst time we had with them and the men had to take their guns with them to work. While one guarded the cattle the others would plow. The Indians only took one child from our settlement and we never got her back.

Once the Indians stole a great many horses from Brother Thatcher, and since my husband was a minute man, he had to go many times without even saying good-bye to look for stolen cattle. We tried to keep a good supply of bread on hand to encourage the Indians to be more friendly towards us. One year they killed a number of settlers north of Logan and the soldiers from Fort Douglas were called and a real battle ensued, the place now being called Battle Creek. Nearly all the Indians were killed and some of the soldiers but we never had any more trouble after this. The soldiers camped on Tabernacle Square, and I sent bread, butter and eggs to eat.

We also had grasshopper wars. I have seen the heavens darkened with grasshoppers until one would think it was midnight. I have gone out at such times and driven them into a trench with a bunch of willows and buried them alive. Even with all we killed the ground would be left perfectly bare of vegetation. They destroyed our crops and my husband had to go over into another valley and work on a threshing machine to get bread for the winter.

On October 18, 1861, my husband took me and his mother and started to Salt Lake City, and on October the 26, 1861 I went to the Endowment House and received my endowments and was sealed to my husband for time and eternity.

A short time before the birth of my first baby I also had my first experience in sewing. My husband had a fine young steer that he was saving to sell in order to get enough money for us to buy material to make clothing for the new little baby we were expecting. One of the prominent brethren of Logan at this time suffered a great financial loss and was destitute. The people were called upon to give what they could for the support of this unfortunate family. We had our winter supply of food in the house, but no money, the steer being held for such a purpose. My husband came home feeling very badly and said, "Margaret, I am very sorry and disappointed but I have been called upon to raise some money to help out one of our brethren, and the only thing I have that I can give is that steer. What shall I do?" My husband's gratitude for my willingness brought him to tears. It was a big sacrifice for us, but we both knew it was right.

After my husband left the house, I hunted out two of his old homespun woolen shirts and pulled down the blinds and locked the doors so that no one would see me try my hand at a new art. I spread the shirts on the floor and, without a pattern, cut out two little dresses and sewed them up by hand. This was practically all the clothes I had for my first child. However, she was most welcome to us and given as much love as two loving parents were capable of bestowing. She was born January 18, 1863. We named her Margaret Hannah, and my husband was the proudest father in the valley.

By 1864 my husband had prospered, and we were able to live very comfortably. In that year, he went with his team in Captain Preston's company to help gather in the poor from the plains before the winter weather came. During his absence I spun and wove a nice big piece of cloth to make our winter clothing. He returned on September 19. On the 20th our first son was born who we named Henry William after his father and grandfather.

My husband had started to build us an adobe house on the corner of our lot. We had been living in a little log house which was later to be our granary. I helped him make the adobes and we were so happy when we were able to move into it just before our next child was born. On Sunday, July, 8, 1866 our son and third child was born. He was named Thomas McNeil Ballard, after my father.

The law of plural marriage had now been made manifest by revelation to the servants of God. My husband being a Bishop had been counseled by the authorities to set the example of obedience by entering in this law. The compliance of this was a greater trial to my husband than it was to me. He would say to me, "Margaret, you are the only woman in the world I ever want. I am satisfied with only you." While this was a trial for us both, we knew that the Lord expected us to be obedient to this law as in all laws as revealed in these latter days.

After many weeks of pondering and praying for guidance, I persuaded my husband to enter into this law and suggested to him my sister, Emily, who was three years younger than myself, as his second wife. This was agreeable to him for she was a beautiful and lovable girl of eighteen years.

During their courtship my husband was manly, dignified, honorable and upright toward me and my sister. Never once did he neglect me or leave me alone during this time. Many times he took me to my mother's with my babies to spend the evening while he took Emily to a dance, and at all times he showed me every consideration and courtesy.

After he had won her love and after he had given her his, he and Emily decided to be married in October. They went to Salt Lake and were married in the Endowment House. Henry asked me to go with them on this trip. I made protest as I was in a delicate condition and thought the trip would be too hard. Henry was grieved and said to me, "Margaret, unless you go with me and give your consent to this marriage and stand as a witness, I will not go." I went and made the trip in a covered wagon over a hundred miles of rough road and gave my consent and blessing to this union.

On October 4, 1867, my husband married my sister Emily as his second wife. Although I loved my sister dearly and we knew it was a commandment of God that we should live in the Celestial Marriage, it was a great trial and sacrifice for me. But the Lord blessed and comforted me and we lived happily in this principle of the Gospel. I have thanked the Lord every day of my life that I have had the privilege of living that law.

After my husband's marriage to Emily, one morning as I awoke, I turned my face to the wall and wept a little and felt very lonely, alone in my condition. I heard a sound and thought someone had come into my room. I turned in my bed and I saw a most beautiful young woman dressed in white. She said to me, "Be of good cheer, I have just brought you two choice spirits." At that moment I felt "life quickening" for the first time of my unborn twins. This was a great comfort to me and I felt that I had been somewhat rewarded for my sacrifice by being blessed with a promise of not one but two more children.

On May 15, 1868, I gave birth to twin babies, a little girl and boy. We named them Janet and Charles. They were two beautiful babies but did not stay long with us on this earth. The little girl died on September 18, 1869, and ten days later the little boy died. This was a very sore trial for me.

During the winter of 1869 we had about one hundred sheep wintering in Clarkston. Since it was a very hard winter, and the snow was very deep, nearly all of them were dying. A man came and told my husband that if he wanted to save any of the sheep, he would have to go at once with a wagon and haul them into shelter.

I told my husband to get another wagon and team and I would drive with him. He did not want me to go, but I insisted for I felt so sorry to lose so many sheep and thought we could have double the number with the two wagons. I also thought I could be company for him on such a long drive. It was very cold. We started very early and it was eleven o'clock when we got home that night. We brought twenty sheep back with us, but about half of them died on the way home. I never will forget the sight of so many sheep lying around dead and dying. It made my heart ache to see the suffering of these animals.

On April 9, 1870, my son George Albert was born. He was a fine, big, healthy boy and brought great happiness to our home. The following September I received a Patriarchal blessing from Brother Charles H. Hyde. This was a very great comfort to me. It promised me many privileges and blessings which have nearly all been fulfilled.

On February 9, 1873, I gave birth to another son whom we named Melvin Joseph. Prior to his birth I had lost my twins in death, and my health was broken. I had the misfortune of having several miscarriages, and during the early stages of pregnancy, I was in danger of losing him also. My heart was broken. I had encouraged my husband to go into polygamy, and by so doing he might rear a large posterity to strengthen Zion. Melvin was carried during a period of great trial in my life; a period of poverty, during a national depression, a season of crop failures, a very severe winter, and during the "underground." I had given birth to six children. Two had been taken in death in their infancy, just ten days apart. Sorrow and sickness had weakened my physical strength. My heart was sore, my arms were empty, for again the life of my unborn child was threatened.

For days and weeks I was bedfast, and I felt in my anguish that the "fruit of my womb was cursed." Like Rachel of old, my heart yearned for a child, and I cried unto the Lord, "Give me children or else I die." My husband had taken the children a block way to see a parade, and while he was gone I raised my trembling body from the bed and crawled and locked the door so that I might pour out my soul to God on my knees in prayer. I called to his remembrance my willingness to bear children; my approval of my husband's marriage to my sister that a greater posterity build up his kingdom in Zion. I supplicated the Lord for his help. I felt that I had done all that was in my power, and I asked to know my standing in his sight.

God hearkened unto my prayer and a comfort was given to me. I saw no person but I heard a voice speak plainly to me saying, "Be of good cheer—your life is acceptable, and you will bear a son who will become an apostle of the Lord Jesus Christ."

In due time my child was born; I did bear a son, my last son. We named him Melvin Joseph, and I know he is a chosen son of God.

His life was ever precious to us, and we both recognized in him a choice spirit. He was also honored by his brothers and sisters, although they did not know of the promise given him, nor did I ever tell him. Melvin was not a robust child and his early life was shielded and protected. Neither was his young life a carefree happy life, for again death entered our home and saddened our lives.

During the summer of 1874, there was an epidemic of scarlet fever in Logan. Many families were severely afflicted with it. My brother, Joseph McNeil, contracted the disease and died on Saturday June 13, 1874, at the age of fourteen and one-half years old. My children all came down with it and were very sick. Our little son George Albert died of it on Tuesday, July 7, 1874. Our daughter Margaret Hannah was sick with the same disease when her little brother died. The day after his death his little body was taken to her bedside for a last farewell on earth. This parting was not for long for she too died six days later. He [George Albert] was buried Wednesday, 8th of July, and Margaret [Hannah] died Monday, July 13, 1874 at the age of nearly twelve years. She was buried the next day, Tuesday, July 14th by her brother.

Thus I had been the mother of seven children with but three remaining—three boys; Henry, Thomas and my baby Melvin. Within ten days we had buried our twins, in less than five years later, within six days we buried our other two dear children. How lonely and empty our home was and sad were our hearts.

Not long after we had buried our children, my son, Henry, was helping his father haul peas from the field. In some way he fell on the pitchfork which ran through his bowels. His father prayed over him at the time and asked the Lord to spare his life until he could get him home. When they brought him in he looked like he was dead. I hurried and made an herb plaster and put his whole body in it. We also offered up a mighty prayer for him. He was again restored to health and we know that is was the power of the Lord that saved him, for at that time we had no doctors to help us.

Just two weeks after this on September 19, 1875, I gave birth to another daughter whom we named Ellen Phoebe. She too was taken from us in her young womanhood. A month later my husband was brought home from the Canyon very sick, suffering with kidney trouble.

The brethren had been in and administered to him, but he was very bad, and we felt he would surely die. I was standing at the foot of his bed and greatly grieved to see him in such agony. Looking at me he said he knew he could die if I would only give him up. A voice came to me and said, "Administer to him," but I was very timid about doing this for the elders had just blessed him. The voice came again and I felt with the priesthood in the house I could not do it. I thought they would think me bold and I was very weak. The voice came to me the third time. Heeding its prompting I put my hands upon his head. The spirit of the Holy Ghost was with me and I was filled with a Divine strength in performing this ordinance. When I finished, my husband had fallen asleep and slept quietly for two hours or more. There are still a number of the brethren living who were in the house at the time and they often speak of this miraculous healing.

On February 8th, 1878, another daughter was born to us. We named her Rebecca Ann. Soon after this my husband's father and mother came to live with us. They were with us for about eight years before their deaths, at which time his father was ninety-six and his mother eighty-six. They were both very feeble and required a great deal of care and attention. I was ever willing to care for them and bestow my affection on them in order to make their lives happy. And I know that they both died blessing me. This has always been a comfort to me.

From the first organization of Relief Society in Cache Valley until 1880, I labored as a teacher, and on December eleventh of that year I was put in as President of this organization in the Second Ward with Sister Barbara Larsen as First Counselor and Sister Susan J. Smith as Second Counselor. Sister Emmeline James was Secretary. I served in this capacity for over thirty years. During these years I tried to do my duty in caring for the sick and comforting the needy.

I have walked for blocks through the deep snow. I have been out in rain and wind in the darkest of nights and in the earliest hours of the morning administering to those who were afflicted, sick, suffering and dying. I have sat up all night time after time with the ill. I have laid out the dead and made their burial clothes. I have mothered orphans, comforted widows and striven to be a peace maker to those in trouble and through it all the Lord has directed me and I have enjoyed His Spirit as my companion in these labors. It comforts me to have done some good to those less fortunate than myself. Many, many times I have neglected my own family and home, but the Lord always came to my rescue.

On December 13, 1881, I gave birth to another daughter and we named her Lettie May. Shortly after this a family by the name of Phister, who lived in our ward, were left orphans. The father had died leaving a wife and six small children. Seven months later the mother gave birth to another baby and died while the baby was very young. After her death, the seven children were brought into my home and stayed until after their mother's funeral. Bishop Hardy of Salt Lake distributed them among different people. I adopted one of the little girls, her name was Lana, and raised her as my own until she was married.

Shortly after the Logan Temple had been dedicated, my father was called to be an officiator there and while in this capacity was taken ill with pneumonia, his life being despaired of. One morning early they sent for me and I hurried down lest I should never see my father alive again. I was not well myself, for I had been suffering with erysipelas and had not been out of the house for a week. I wrapped up sufficiently and was taken in a sleigh. When I arrived, Mother was feeling very bad and could not be comforted. When I looked at Father and saw his condition, I was sorrowful myself for you could hear him breathe all over the house. The Spirit of the Lord was with me and I had a desire to administer to him. I asked mother if he had been blessed as yet, and she said that he had that morning. I was timid again about going ahead and doing anything of this sort, but I knew that I should so I asked mother if she did not want to assist me but, she declined because she felt it would be of little use. If the Priesthood had not helped, then she deemed it useless for us to try. I hesitated, but something said to me. "Administer to him," so I went and closed the door and asked mother if she would not pray with me. She consented, and we knelt by the bed and prayed, and I then anointed my father and administered to him. The power of the Lord was with me for while my hands were still on his head, his breathing became much easier. When I finished father opened his eyes and said, "Thank God for this blessing. I knew this power was in the church and I thank Him for it."

This was most wonderful to me and surely the Lord did bless us all. Father was still very weak but that night he sat up in his chair with his clothes on. It was not long after that until he had fully recovered from his sickness. I have told you these experiences so show how perfectly my patriarchal blessing had been fulfilled. I had been promised that I should heal the sick through the Power of the Lord.

I gave birth to another daughter, Mary Myrtle, on August 21, 1885.

It was not until I received my husband's first letter [from London] that I learned to read and write. Up to this time I could do neither, but I was determined to learn to read his letters and to answer them. After many difficulties and obstacles I was able to do both.

While my husband was away, my family had worked very hard, but we were blessed and got along very well. The boys hauled logs from the canyon and sold them, thus helping to support us. Every Sunday we fasted and prayed to the Lord to prosper Brother Ballard in his labors. Through all my trials I was thankful that the Lord did not forget us.

There was a brother who had a plural wife. She was about to be confined. As polygamists we were watched very closely. He feared that the coming of the child would be the cause of his arrest. He went to Apostle Merrill for advice and was told, "You are as near to the Lord as I, go to Him." This man fasted and prayed. When he was in one of the upper rooms of the Temple he heard a voice say, "Take her to Margaret Ballard's" He came to me and told me that he had been sent but did not tell me who sent him. Neither did he tell me whose wife he was asking me to take. We were all willing to help those in trouble so I told him I would do my best to take care of her. She was with me one week before her baby was born. The midwife and I were alone with her, but she got along well and I kept her and her baby for six months and no one molested us. When the man told me how he happened to come to me, it made my heart rejoice to know that my Father in Heaven had such confidence in me.

Because of my husband's being away the deputies did not bother my home and I sheltered a number of the polygamist brethren under my roof and gave them women's clothes to dress in so they might visit their families after dark. I also drove them in my buggy, dressed in disguise to visit their loved ones. They felt safe and the Lord preserved them from attack. It was a laughable sight, sometimes, to see the men dressed in my clothes. We had to pull and push to get them in and leave part unbuttoned then put a shawl around their shoulders to cover up the gapping spaces. Brother Larson was quite stout, and Brother Amuson was a tall thin man, but I would do the best I could and put a hat on their heads, a heavy veil over their faces and tuck them in the buggy with a robe over their lap and drive them after dark to their homes to see their families.

While my husband was in London, he met a sister that was in the under-ground. She had a baby girl and wanted to come back to Utah. My husband wrote and asked me if I would take her in my home. I did so and she stayed with me for a long time and was not molested, so I felt blessed once more.

My husband secured a great deal of genealogy while he was in England and sent these records home to me. My son Henry and I did the work for these names in the Temple. When my husband came back he was very pleased to know that all of the work was done. It gave me great joy to be an instrument in the hands of the Lord in working out the salvation for those who had died in darkness. Again I felt I had fulfilled, in part, another blessing which was promised me by one of God's patriarchs.

In 1887, while my husband was away, my dear father was summoned to serve a sentence of six months in the penitentiary and was fined $100.00. He was at this time counselor to the bishop of the third ward, and all the Saints grieved for him. This was a great trial to me to have my noble father thus abused. They shaved off his long beard and put him in stripes. He took a severe cold and was very sick and was never strong again. He entered January 3, 1887, and was released July 7, 1887.

Brother Ballard was away on his mission for over two years. He arrived home in Logan January of 1889. In order that he might not be detected, he took a freight train from Salt Lake City and traveled in the night, arriving home in the early morning. I did not know just when to expect him, but I felt impressed that he would come in this manner and sat up all night waiting for him. When I heard the train whistling into Mendon, I awakened my son Thomas and sent him to the station to meet his father. He arrived safely but did not know Thomas because he had grown so much during the separation. Although our meeting was held in secrecy, it was a joyful one. We were thankful for the work my husband had been able to accomplish, for his protection, and for the health we had all been granted during his absence.

After Brother Ballard had been home for a few days, he thought it best to go to the officers and tell them he was ready to serve his term for polygamy. The officers granted him a day to rest and visit his families. Then he went to Ogden and was tried before a court, fined fifty dollars and sentenced to two months imprisonment. He paid the fine and served his term and then returned to us feeling free from this obligation.

The following December my little daughter Ellen took sick with membranous croup. She suffered terribly for several days and then died, the date being December 13,

1889. She was fourteen years old and a great comfort to me and such a companion during her father's absence. Of course it was another severe blow to us. the Lord gave me strength so that I came to know that it was best that she should be taken.

Ten days before her death I had a dream which troubled me greatly for I knew it concerned the children whom I had buried. After her death I went to the Temple to get endowments for her and was feeling very badly. I prayed that I might understand the meaning of my dream. I was sitting wondering why I had been called to go through this sacrifice once more when the interpretation of my dream went before my eyes. With great plainness I saw that which would have come upon my children if they had lived. They would have been lost to me. I saw my five beautiful children saved for me and knew that they would be mine again. I had this vision, for which I feel thankful, and this is as true as the sun ever shines upon the earth.

On March 8, 1891, my son Henry was called to be Bishop of the Benson Ward. He was set apart by Apostle Moses Thatcher and he held this position for over twenty years.

In the fall of 1891 my father took sick and died suddenly. This was another sorrow for me for I loved him dearly and felt his loss keenly. I relied upon him in trouble and sickness and felt that I had truly lost a good friend and loving father. His life had always been an inspiration to me as well as a guiding star.

On April 6, 1893, I attended the dedication of the Salt Lake Temple. My soul was filled with joy for the privilege of being a partaker of such a Heavenly feast as was manifested at that dedication

A few weeks after his marriage Melvin went upon his first mission. During his absence I gave his wife a home with me and did everything I could for her welfare and comfort. While she was with me she gave birth to their son Melvin Russell. He was a very delicate child and we had many serious times to pass through with him. The Lord was good to us and answered our prayers and restored him many times to health. Day after day I fasted and prayed for him. Surely the Lord was good to spare his life.

My mother died December 6, 1900, after an illness that had lasted over two years. During her sickness I endeavored to render willing service for her benefit. She lived with my sister Jeannette about three blocks from my home. Every day during those two years I walked back and forth two or three times a day to assist my sister, who had very poor health herself, to care for my mother. It grieved me to see my mother afflicted for such a long time. I did everything I could to comfort her, and in turn I received her gratitude and blessing.

March 13, 1901, my sister Jeannette died leaving five orphan children, three boys and two girls. Her husband had died two years previously. Upon her death bed she pleaded with me to take her two little girls and raise them as my own. After the funeral I brought the two little girls, Edna, aged six, and Jeannette, aged ten to my home. I have done my duty by them as well as I have known how, and I know my Heavenly Father is satisfied with my efforts. Now they are raised I am proud to have had a part in their upbringing. I love them and know that they love me.

My sister Emily took sick about this time and suffered severely for months. This was another trial for me for, although we had many misunderstandings and differences of opinion, she was very dear to me. We had traveled the road together for many years and passed through trials and hardships together. We had stood by each other in all experiences of life. While we had our difficulties, living the law of plural marriage, I believe we lived it and got along as well as human beings could be expected to live it. I know we will have cause for great rejoicing in the Hereafter for having done so well.

After her death I tried to do justice to her children in all of our dealings. I have endeavored to give motherly counsel and advice to them all, both sons and daughters, sons-in-law and daughters-in-law. I love them every one next to my very own, and I know they love me for they always have shown me affection and respect.

My husband died February 26, 1908, after a brief illness. He had been suffering for a number of years and I was thankful that he was released. My life was more lonely without him than anyone can imagine without having experienced it themselves. He was a kind and loving husband, an affectionate father, a man of honor and justice, filled with faith in God and exercised great power in his Priesthood. I have been a widow for nine years and yet each day I miss him more and know that I will be filled with joy when I am once more associated with him.

Five months after their marriage D. Ray went on a mission to England. During his absence my daughter made her home with me for the greater part of the time. In this way I have assisted the spread of the Gospel by providing a home and food for my three daughters and one daughter-in-law while their husbands have taken the Gospel to the nations of the world. I have given what material aid I could to help along with this work so near and dear to my heart. A number of my grandsons have also filled missions and for this I am thankful.

My son Melvin was called to preside over the Northwestern States Mission shortly after his father's death. He left in April 1909 and is still laboring in this capacity. He has been an instrument in performing a great work. I have visited him a number of times in Portland Oregon during his mission. It has been my happy lot to minister unto several of the Elders in this part of the Lord's field. I learned to love them all because of the work which they represent. I have gone out to their street meetings and raised my voice in defense of the truth and have borne my testimony of the truthfulness of this work to throngs of people crowded in the streets of Portland. My heart rejoices for this great privilege and I thank God for the testimony which I was able to bear on such occasions. In my weak way I feel that I have assisted in the spread of truth and am grateful for this opportunity.

I am thankful for my family, for their love and respect and for the honor they have always shown to their father and me. I appreciate their obedience and am happy in their desire to follow their parents example, concerning the things of the Lord. I feel blessed that they have all had the privilege of having been married in the Temple by the Priesthood of God and sealed for time and eternity—not just my family but all of my husband's children, and also those whom I have raised as my own.

My life has been one of varied experiences. I have had a great deal of sickness to pass through, both with my children and grandchildren, but I have always relied upon the Lord and He has never failed me. I have stood by my husband through sickness, trials, poverty and prosperity. I have labored by his side in the fields. I have done various types of work such as soap making, weaving, spinning, reaping, sowing, plowing and gleaning. From the very first day I entered this valley until this day I have never ceased my labors to up build and beautify this city.

Although my life has been one of sacrifice and service I feel that I have lived it the best I could with the knowledge I have had. My testimony of the truthfulness of the Gospel grows stronger each day, and the work grows dearer and sweeter to my soul. I know that God lives and that He lives and answers prayers, that Jesus is the Son of The Living God and that Joseph Smith was His Prophet. I thank God for this knowledge and leave this as my testimony to my children and grandchildren and all who may come after me. I plead of you all to heed the Spirit of God that you may also have this testimony burning in your hearts that you may have his Spirit as your daily companion.

EPILOGUE BY FAMILY MEMBERS

The foregoing autobiography was written about one year before her death. Her last year, like all other years of her full life was spent in service and devotion to her religion, her country and her family.

Shortly after her return to Logan from the April conference of 1918 she was afflicted with high blood pressure which resulted in slow hemorrhages of the brain. During the ten weeks which it lasted, she suffered intensely without complaint or murmur. From the day she was forced to take to her bed until the last breath of life she accepted whatever came as the will of the Father with such resignation as is rarely found.

Because she had a strong constitution, her family felt that there was no reason that she should not survive this illness and live many more years. But she was firm in her conviction that she was not to remain. She would say, "I am satisfied with my life as I have lived it and I am ready to go back."

Those who were privileged to be with her during her last sickness received the benefit of the golden hours of her well-spent life. Her mind was keen and bright to the last, sensitive to her appearance and to her surroundings.

It has been said that some people walk and talk with God. Her faith was such and her belief so personal that surely she was among these people whose sincerity is thus rewarded with the certainty that there is a definite plan for all things and a definite place in that plan for each.

To those who knew and remember her, one of the outstanding attributes of her character they believe should be emphasized was her love for her husband. He was a large lovable man, sincere and deliberate. She was energetic, a noble little soul. Their characters complimented each other. He protected her and was her refuge. She inspired and companioned his every activity. Typical of his devotion and dependence upon her was the crisis they both met when he was asked to take another wife. When he felt he should do as suggested, he came to her and said, "Margaret, I do not want any other woman but you. If I must, you will have to find her for me." She did.

Her determination was second only to her faith, and an integral part of her. Typical of its expression was the remodeling of her house which was done when she was approaching seventy. She had asked her sons to help her remove a very bothersome partition in a closet in order to make a sitting room more spacious. Her sons agreed to do it for her, and as busy people will, put off doing so. Surprised at the change in her house some time later when her oldest son came to see her he asked if the other brother had done it. "No," she firmly replied. "Well, who did it then?" was the rejoinder. "I did it myself." When her son asked her why she hadn't let him help, she grew ruffled and replied, "I did ask you, you know."

The patriarchal blessing that she refers to during her life was given to her at the time she was carrying her youngest son, Melvin. She was sad and somewhat depressed at the time. She has repeated most of it in her story, but one part that was omitted was denied her at the time of her death. She was promised that the child she was bearing would grow to become one of the leaders of the Church and that his power of good would be felt by many. Perhaps she hesitated to insert this promise until it had been fulfilled. The joy that she would have known had she lived but a few months to realize that her unbounded faith would find its outlet in her youngest son, Melvin, who was inspired not only from himself, but from her too.

She died on a beautiful Sunday morning July 21, 1918, at seventy-two years of age. She was the mother of eleven children, six of whom she raised. She had numerous grandchildren and great grandchildren. Her funeral was held in the Logan Tabernacle and was one of simplicity and peace, so typical of her life. She was buried beside her husband in the Logan Cemetery, one spot on earth very dear to her heart.

EMILY

Emily's life paralleled the life of her sister Margaret in many ways. She was born in Tranent, Heddingtonshire, Scotland, on June 19, 1849, and was baptized a member of the LDS Church in 1857 at the age of eight.

Her trip to America, and subsequently to Utah, was a lot like Margaret's although she was spared the burden of carrying her little brother across the prairie.

The trip was not a direct one—two years were spent in Genoa, and more time was spent at Woodriver. Both towns were in Nebraska.

When the McNeils left Woodriver in the summer of 1859, they came directly west to Utah. They were advised to go down Weber Canyon to Ogden and bypass Salt Lake City to save time—it was October 4, 1859, when they reached Ogden. There they met Henry Ballard and his friend, Aaron DeWitt and traveled to Cache Valley with them.

Cache Valley was well settled when they arrived, and it was impossible to secure the best land. Since they had to live off the land, the McNeils settled on a farm west of Logan.

It was hard to make a living anywhere in Cache Valley, and in the West Field it was even more difficult. All members of the family had to work or starve, and they were required to work almost beyond their strength. Thomas, though only thirteen years old, worked in the fields alongside his father. His ability and willingness to work impressed Brother Ricks, and Thomas was hired to plow his fields. The family needed the extra income, and Margaret, though only one year older than Thomas, was required to replace him. After Margaret's marriage to Henry Ballard, Brother McNeil felt Emily would have to take Margaret's place in the field.

Thomas, in the meantime, had returned home to work, and seeing how hard Emily was forced to labor spoke to his father about it. He threatened to leave the farm if Emily, only eleven, had to continue working like a man. Brother McNeil, realizing his son was serious, sent Emily to the kitchen to help her mother. Emily disliked field work intensely and remembered Thomas's kindness until her dying day.

Emily grew to young womanhood both pretty and popular. She had many pursuers and many chances to marry or to join in plural marriage—she shunned all of them.

When Henry Ballard approached her to ask for her hand in marriage as his second wife, she gave it serious consideration. After much prayer and fasting she accepted Henry's proposal.

With Margaret as a witness, Emily was sealed to Henry in the Salt Lake City Endowment House on October 4, 1867. The three were now partners in plural marriage.

When they returned to Logan, Emily moved into the Ballard home and had a room to herself. At first she and Margaret worked side by side sharing housework, but later on taking turns seemed more practical.

Henry built a two-room addition for Emily, and she was alone for a time, but on February 12, 1870, Henry noted in his journal:

> My wife Emily bore me a little daughter[,] we named her Elizabeth[,] she [Emily] got along well

Elizabeth was a delicate child from her birth and at the age of five months passed away.

In the fall of 1871 Henry and Robert Davidson took a small contract to help in the building of the railroad in Box Elder County. Near the end of October Henry took Emily along to cook for his men. The work was difficult, the cold extreme, and the tents that housed them offered scant shelter from the elements. Supplies were also running low.

Henry left for Logan on November 25 to get more supplies. A short time after he returned home a storm struck that threatened his return trip with the much-needed food. On November 27, he started back to Box Elder County knowing that Emily and his men would be cold, hungry, and anxious. The severity of the storm and a broken leg from a previous accident forced Henry to turn back to Logan. Fortunately, another group of men forced their way through and brought Emily safely home.

On November 26, 1872, Emily bore Henry a son. They named him Willard Russell Ballard.

The crowded conditions in the two rooms prompted Henry to build a small home on the south half of his Logan lot. It was in this house Emily's next three children were born—the first of the three being Franklin, who arrived on November 28, 1874.

Emily loved the beautiful and delicate things in life. Her hands were skilled, as was her mind, and she offered classes in which she taught flower making and hat braiding. The money generated from the sale of these products and the fees charged for classes were used to beautify her home both inside and out.

Supportive of Henry, Emily was among the first to be baptized into the United Order in 1875.

The following year her fourth child, Ernest Reid, was born on October 20, 1876, and was blessed by his grandfather McNeil.

Her son, Franklin, when three years old, contracted rheumatic fever, and it appeared he would not survive. His grandfather gave him a blessing and ordained him an elder of the Church—customary in these circumstances at the time. Following the blessing Franklin improved and eventually recovered, but he suffered from the effects of the disease for the rest of his life.

When the Logan Temple was dedicated in May of 1884, Emily was there—she did a great deal of work for her kindred dead in the temple.

In 1877 Henry hauled lumber to Cache Junction to build section houses for the working railroad hands, and he bought land on which to build a United Order dairy. The dairy would one day profoundly affect Emily's life.

Emily's next child, Lydia Jane, was born on September 9, 1878. Two years later, on November 4, 1880, Jennie Lulu Ballard was born. Henry didn't have a chance to bless her until the following January 6, 1881.

In the spring of 1882 Henry homesteaded ground near Cache Junction, and a summer home was built on the "ranch." Emily spent many summers on the banks of the Bear River at the ranch. Sometimes she stayed in a section house near the dairy in Cache Junction. During the winter months she returned to Logan where her children could attend school and have the benefits of a warm place to live.

During those years the federal agents were relentless in their efforts to arrest Henry, or any other polygamist they could. Many were the times Henry slipped through a trapdoor in the floor of the ranch house and Emily would replace the rug and bed that had covered it. Often the damp earth under the house was Henry's only defense against arrest. Emily was left to deal with the officers as best she could. She was often subpoenaed before a grand jury and quizzed about Henry and their plural marriage.

Polygamy created problems for her children as well. They had to be constantly on the alert for the deputies and told many "white lies" to protect Henry. He was not free to mingle with the family, but had to sleep and eat in a small storeroom that had been added to the back of the house. It was always his daughter Jennie's job to take his meals to him and to see that he was provided for.

On one occasion Emily's son Willard was helping his father with the plowing. The sun came out, and it was rather warm, so to be more comfortable Henry took his coat off and hung it on the plow handle. Suddenly, seemingly out of nowhere, the deputies appeared coming down the road in a White Top buggy. Not wanting to be seen, Henry ran to the river and hid himself in the brush. Noticing Henry's coat, Willard hurriedly put it on the ground in front of the plow, and gave the horses a sharp rap with the whip. The plow covered up the coat with the earth, and no evidence of Henry was to be was found. Once more Henry escaped the long arm of law.

Amy Eugine, Emily's seventh and last child, was born January 23, 1885.

By then the United Order dairy was in full swing. About twenty girls had been hired to do the milking, and two young men were employed to feed and herd the cows. During the summers Emily took her young family to the dairy. She lived in the section house and helped with the cooking and the manufacture of cheese and butter. With one hundred head of cows it was a busy place. When the United Order was dissolved, Henry and Robert Davidson bought the dairy and operated it as a joint venture. Later they divided their interests and operated two dairies—Emily never wanted for something to do.

In Logan one winter, word reached the Ballards that some people who had settled in Newton were planning to slip across the river as soon as it froze and "jump" Henry's homestead claim. Emily lost no time in reacting and moved quickly to the ranch with all the supplies she could get.

It was a particularly cold, stormy, and lonely winter. Emily and her children saw no other people for weeks at a time. Their only company was the howl of the marauding coyotes that preyed on what little livestock they had. Sometimes her twelve-year-old son, Willard, would fire his rifle into the night sky to quiet the roaming animals so the family could get some sleep.

Emily wanted her family to learn, and she became their teacher in all things, including prayers and worship. Sundays were observed with reverence, and they dressed in the best clothes they had. During those long winter evenings Emily taught the children reading, writing, and arithmetic.

The people who planned on "jumping" the Ballard claim were no match for this courageous woman.

When Henry's persecutions become unbearable, he decided to go on a mission to England. However, he could not give assistance to Emily or Margaret while he was gone—they would have to assist him. This decision, which Emily supported, left them in dire circumstances.

After his mission, persecution resumed, and Henry considered taking Emily and her family to live with him in southern Canada. Margaret suggested it as an alternative to what they were going through. It was Emily who said no. She felt she had no right to take Henry from Margaret and the rest of his family. It would have been much easier for her than what lay ahead, but Emily felt it was wrong.

Henry eventually divided all his property between his two wives. Emily received the property in Newton and Cache Junction. The time finally came when Emily would live out the rest of her life there, without Henry, except as his health would permit him to visit and help when he could.

Union Pacific planned to lay tracks through Cache Junction, and in the spring of 1890 the surveying was completed. The tracks were to pass through the Ballard farm. The company bought a right-of-way from Emily and some additional property large enough for a railroad station in Cache Junction. Emily decided to open a boardinghouse and eating establishment for railroad employees and passengers who traveled through Cache Junction.

Emily had no money, so she borrowed it from her brother, Hyrum. Henry did the things he could do. With his youngest son, Melvin J., he hauled lumber from Logan to build the boardinghouse. He also rocked up a well for her.

The dry clay soil surrounding what had now become Emily's new home was completely bereft of trees and water. Emily planted trees and watered them by hand from the well Henry had rocked up for her.

The boardinghouse did quite well, but it was very demanding—consuming seven days of every week. Emily was cooking for about twenty section hands as well as the railroad passengers that came through Cache Junction. The meals included huge trays of meats and vegetables, and everyone was invited to eat their fill for $.50 per meal. Lydia and Jennie, thirteen and eleven years of age, waited on the tables. Little Amy, age six, was left to attend to herself. Later, at an early age, Amy also helped with the dishes and the table waiting.

The boys, Willard, Frank and Ernest, were kept busy chopping wood for the cookstove so the meals could continue. In addition they also ran the farm. There was little leisure time for Emily or her children.

In 1892 Emily bought a building that had once housed a tavern. She donated it to the community for a school. A teacher was hired, and Emily's children attended the school.

The distance to Cache Junction was not as great as the family bonds of love. Since Emily was so tied to the station, Margaret often brought her family to Emily's for visits, family reunions, and sometimes to spend the holidays. The interaction between the two families was one of love and friendship, and the relationship continued for many years.

Emily Elizabeth had died in infancy, and Amy passed away, probably from a ruptured appendix, when she was sixteen years old. The rest of the family were married in the temple, and the boys filled honorable missions.

The years passed quickly for Emily, but her body was consumed by cancer in her later years. Emily was only 54 years old when she passed into a better world on May 7, 1903. Before her death she had asked to be buried in the Newton Cemetery beside her beloved Amy.

The 25 years that Emily was married to Henry had been full of trials, but there were good times as well.

Emily suffered—but she suffered in silence—spurning the help of doctors. Many of her trials would have broken an ordinary person, but she took everything in stride and did the best she could with what she had.

The family Emily left behind stands as a monument to her love and devotion to them and to all human beings. Her unwavering adherence to the principal of doing good for everyone she ever met has made her a worthy example that anyone would do well to follow.

May the role played by this remarkable pioneer woman always be remembered by those of us who follow.

Left to right, top: Rebecca, Melvin J., Henry William, Tom
Bottom: Letti, Margaret, Myrtle, Ellen

Left to right: Lydia, Willard, Emily, Amy, Jennie, Frank, Ernest

Henry and Margaret's Family

Margaret Hannah ....died at age eleven.

Henry William ....married Elvira Day Davidson.

Thomas McNeil .... married Phoebe John Smith.

Charles James ....died age sixteen months.

Janet McNeil....................................died age sixteen months.

Geroge Albert .... died at age four.

Melvin Joseph ....married Martha Annabele Jones.

Ellen Pheobe ....died at age fourteen.

Rebecca Ann ....married Louis Samuel Cardon.

Lettie May .... married George Washington Squires.

Mary Myrtle .... married Daniel Ray Shurtliff.

Henry and Emily's Family

Emily Elizabeth ....died age six months.

Willard Russell ....married Bessie Griffin.

Franklin Hyrum ....married Sarah Stevens.

Ernest Reid ....married Amanda Miller.

Lydia Jane .... married William Henry Griffin.

Jennie Lulu ....married Franklin Thomas Griffin.

Amy Eugine ....died at age sixteen.

INDEX

Index

Index